withdrawn

A BIBLIOGRAPHY OF THE WORKS OF

LOUIS MACNEICE

BBC Copyright Photograph

A Bibliography of the Works of

LOUIS MACNEICE

by
C. M. ARMITAGE
and
NEIL CLARK

KAYE & WARD
LONDON

First published by Kaye & Ward Ltd 1973
Copyright © 1973 Kaye & Ward Ltd

All Rights Reserved. No part of this publication may be reproduced, stored in a retrieval system, or transmitted, in any form or by any means, electronic, mechanical, photocopying, recording or otherwise, without the prior permission of the copyright owner.

ISBN 0 7182 0934 6

All enquiries and requests relevant to this title should be sent to the publisher Kaye & Ward Ltd., 21 New Street, London EC2M 4NT, and not to the printer.

Printed in England by
C. Tinling & Co. Ltd.
London and Prescot

CONTENTS

Preface		7
Section		
A	Books by Louis MacNeice	9
B	Contributions to Books and Periodicals	61
C	Selective List of Books and Articles about MacNeice	85
D	Miscellanea	105
	(1) Collections of his manuscripts	107
	(2) MacNeice's scripts in the Radio Play Library of the BBC	108
	(3) Gramophone recordings of his poems	113
E	Index of Poems	115
General Index		133

PREFACE

THIS bibliography has been jointly compiled by two enthusiasts for MacNeice's writings. After gathering data independently for several years, we became aware of each other's efforts and thought co-operation a worthier procedure than a competitive race to beat each other into print. We hope that this book will be useful to scholars and admirers of MacNeice.

Our being situated on opposite sides of the Atlantic has had disadvantages but has at least enabled the tracking down of remote items which defied finding from afar. Inevitably, however, some items will have eluded us; we would be grateful for information about them. Various kinds of information have proved unobtainable: for example, attempts to ascertain which of the columns entitled "London Diary" in *The New Statesman* were written by Louis MacNeice drew a blank even from the writer of the history of that periodical; some publishers of books by MacNeice either no longer have or are unwilling to supply statistics about them; most libraries do not keep dust-jackets; and so on. Moreover, the requirement to establish terminal dates for the different sections of the Bibliography has necessarily led to the omission of such recently published items as D. B. Moore's book *The Poetry of Louis MacNeice* (Leicester University Press, 1972).

Section A describes the books by MacNeice and the book he co-authored with W. H. Auden, *Letters from Iceland*. Section B lists MacNeice's contributions to books and periodicals. Section C is a selective list of books and articles about MacNeice. Section D, 'Miscellanea,' lists (1) collections of his MSS, (2) his scripts in the Radio Play Library of the British Broadcasting Corporation, and (3) Gramophone recordings of his poems. Section E is an alphabetical list of his published poems, showing their publishing history, including changes of title: this section has been compiled solely by Neil Clark.

In Section A, detail has been kept to a minimum consistent with positive identification of each edition. The term 'American issue' is used for those books imported from Great Britain and differing from the English editions only in binding and title-page. The size of volumes is given to the nearest half-centimetre. The colours correspond to those in *Colours for Specific Purposes* (British Standards Institution publication B.S. 381C: 1964), though occasionally the colour of a book did not exactly match any illustrated in that publication; and after the first citation of a colour, e.g., 'Deep Brunswick Green', it is shortened to 'green' if it is referred to again in that entry. The standard abbreviations are used, with the addition that, in the listings of contents, (p) means poem.

We would like to acknowledge the help of many people, including: Mrs. Hedli MacNeice; Professor E. R. Dodds; Mr. B. C. Bloomfield; Mr. Ian Hamilton; Mr. John Hilton; Mr. John Johnson; Professor Edward Mendelson; Mr. Charles Monteith; Mrs. Elizabeth Ogilvie; Mr. R. D. Smith; Mr. W. A. Taylor; Mr. R. F. Willetts.

We also wish to thank the following librarians: Miss Kay Hutchings and Miss Hilary Paul of the BBC Radio Play Library; Miss Florence Blakely of Duke University Library; Mrs. Pattie McIntyre of the University of North Carolina Library; Mrs. Mary Hirth of the University of Texas Library; the staffs of Birmingham Public Library; Cardiff Public Library; Kensington and Chelsea Public Library; Morley College Library; New York Public Library; The Poetry Society Library.

The following publishers kindly supplied information: Aldus Books; Appleton-Century-Crofts; Basil Blackwell; Cambridge University Press; The Clarendon Press; Doubleday; Faber and Faber; Victor Gollancz; Harcourt Brace Jovanovich; H. M. Stationery Office; Michael Joseph; Longmans; The New Statesman; The Observer; G. P. Putnam; The Oxford University Press; Random House; The Review.

We are also grateful to Mr. John Hilton for the loan of material for illustrations.

C. M. Armitage	Neil Clark, A.L.A.
University of North Carolina	London

A
BOOKS BY LOUIS MACNEICE
TERMINAL DATE: DECEMBER 1970

A1 BLIND FIREWORKS 1929

First edition:
LOUIS MACNEICE | *Blind Fireworks* | LONDON | VICTOR GOLLANCZ | 14 Henrietta Street Covent Garden | 1929

Collation: 19×13 cm. A^8 B–E^8 (gatherings B–E also signed F) 40 leaves pp1–4 5–80

p1 half-title p2 To GIOVANNA p3 title-page p4 *Printed in Great Britain by* | The Camelot Press Ltd., London and Southampton pp5–6 Foreword pp7–80 text.

Black cloth binding, verdigris green label affixed to head of spine, black lettering across: BLIND | FIRE- | WORKS | LOUIS | MACNEICE.

Cream laid paper, foredge leaves untrimmed.

1,000 copies printed. Published March 1929, price 6/-.

Contents:
Inaugural rant—Reminiscences of infancy—Child's terror—Child's Unhappiness—A conventional serenade—Spring—The universe—Poussin—A serene evening—Gardener melancholy—Sailor's funeral—A cataract conceived as the march of corpses—Corpse carousal—Sunset—A night—Neurotics—Happy families—Song in the back of the mind—Bound in stupidity and unbound—Homo sum—The court historian—This tournament—A lame idyll—Coal and fire—Falling asleep—The humorous atheist addresses his humorous maker—Cynicism—The sunset conceived as a peal of bells—Candle poems (I and II)—Glass falling—ΓΝΩΘΙ ΣΕΑYTON—Adonis—Old maid—Harvest thanksgiving—A classical education—Evening indoors (I and II)—Senescence—The lugubrious, salubrious seaside—The sea—Middle-age—Beginning of a comic-delirious drama—Impermanent creativeness—Adam's legacy—Twilight of the gods

A2 ROUNDABOUT WAY 1932

First edition:
Louis Malone | ROUNDABOUT WAY | PUTNAM | [swelled rule] | LONDON & NEW YORK

Collation: 19×13 cm. A^4 B–S^8 140 leaves pp$i$–*viii* 1–270 *271–272* pp*i–ii* blank p*iii* half-title p*iv* blank p*v* title-page p*vi* *Printed in Great Britain by* | THE SHENVAL PRESS p*vii* *To my Wife* | *who has the gift of* | *enjoying and so will* | *(I hope) enjoy this* | *unheroic story* p*viii* blank pp*1–270* text pp*271–272* blank.

Aircraft blue plastic binding, gold lettering stamped across spine: ROUND- | ABOUT | WAY | LOUIS | MALONE | PUTNAM.
Cream laid paper, foredge and lower edge leaves untrimmed.

Publisher has no record of number of copies printed. Published October 1932, price 7/6.

A3 POEMS 1935

First edition:
LOUIS MACNEICE | POEMS | FABER AND FABER

Collation: 22 × 14.5 cm. A^8 $B-C^8$ D^{10} 34 leaves pp*1–8 9 10–12 13–66 67–68*
p*1* half-title p*2* blank p*3* title-page p*4* PRINTED IN GREAT BRITAIN BY | R. MACLEHOSE AND COMPANY LIMITED | THE UNIVERSITY PRESS GLASGOW p*5* To My Wife p*6* blank p*7* Acknowledgments p*8* blank p*9* Contents p*10* blank p*11* διώκει παῖς ποτανὸν ὄρνιν. ('like a boy who chases a flying bird' Agamemnon, 374) p*12* blank pp*13–66* text pp*67–68* blank.

Light orange cloth binding, gold lettering stamped down spine: Poems—Louis MacNeice Faber and Faber.
White wove paper, foredge and lower edge leaves untrimmed.
6,691 copies printed. Published September 1935, price 6/-.
2nd imp. December 1937; 3rd imp. November 1941; 4th imp. May 1945

Contents:
An eclogue for Christmas—Valediction—Eclogue by a five-barred gate—Morning sun—Turf stacks—The individualist speaks—Train to Dublin—Cuckoo—The creditor—Perseus—To a communist—Sunday morning—Intimations of mortality—Birmingham—Nature morte—Upon this beach—Snow—Belfast—An April manifesto—A contact—Insidiae—Wolves—August—Aubade—The glacier—Spring voices—Museums—Spring sunshine—Circe—Trapaeze—Mayfly—Ode

A4a THE AGAMEMNON OF AESCHYLUS 1936

First edition:
THE AGAMEMNON | OF | AESCHYLUS | *translated by* | Louis MacNeice | Faber and Faber Limited | 24 *Russell Square* | London

Collation: 22.5 × 14.5 cm. A^8 B–D^8 E^4 36 leaves pp*1*–6 7–71 72

p*1* half-title p*2* one work by LM p*3* title-page p*4* *Printed in Great Britain by* | *R. MacLehose and Company Limited* | *The University Press Glasgow* p*5* To | MY FATHER p*6* blank pp7–9 Preface p*10* blank p*11* Characters p*12* blank pp13–71 text p*72* blank.

Dark violet cloth binding, gold lettering stamped down spine: *Agamemnon of Aeschylus Louis MacNeice F & F.*
White wove paper, fore and lower edge leaves untrimmed.
2nd and 3rd imps. printed by Bradford and Dickens, Drayton House, London W.C.1. Both imps. cased in signal red cloth binding. Gold lettering stamped down spine: *The Agamemnon of Aeschylus—Louis MacNeice* F & F. Dustjacket 2nd imp. French grey flecked with blue. Red lettering, front cover: THE | AGAMEMNON | OF AESCHYLUS | translated | by LOUIS | MACNEICE | Faber & Faber. Spine lettering: THE AGAMEMNON OF AESCHYLUS translated by LOUIS MACNEICE FABER AND FABER. Publisher's list on back of jacket. Dustjacket 3rd imp. French grey flecked with blue. Red lettering, front cover: [key meander pattern] | THE | AGAMEMNON | OF | AESCHYLUS | [pattern as above] | translated by | LOUIS | MACNEICE. Spine lettering: [key meander pattern] AGAMEMNON OF AESCHYLUS [pattern as above] MACNEICE (then across spine) F & F [pattern as above]. Publisher's list on back of jacket.

2,000 copies printed. Published October 1936, price 5/-.
2nd imp. 1951; 3rd imp. March 1955

Notes: First produced by the Group Theatre at the Westminster Theatre, November 1 and 8, production and choreography by Rupert Doone, music by Benjamin Britten, and masks and costumes designed by Robert Medley.

A4b THE AGAMEMNON OF AESCHYLUS 1937

First American issue:
THE AGAMEMNON | OF | AESCHYLUS | *translated by* | Louis MacNeice | *New York* | Harcourt, Brace and Company

Collation: as first edition

Contents: as first edition *but* p4 *Made and Printed in Great Britain*

Beige cloth binding, black lettering stamped down spine: THE AGAMEMNON OF AESCYHLUS HARCOURT, BRACE | AND COMPANY. White wove paper.

Later impressions as above *but* p3 title-page; THE AGAMEMNON | OF | AESCHYLUS | *translated by* | Louis MacNeice | Harcourt, Brace and Company | New York. Also p4 *Printed in Great Britain*

260 copies imported from Faber and Faber December 1936, published 25 March 1937, price $1.75.

250 copies imported February 1951, published 26 July 1951, price $2.50.

174 copies imported June 1954, published 1 October 1954, price $3.00.

A4c   AGAMEMNON OF AESCHYLUS   1967

Second English impression:
THE AGAMEMNON | OF | AESCHYLUS | translated by | Louis MacNeice | Faber and Faber Limited | 24 Russell Square | London

Collation: 18 × 12 cm. Perfect binding 36 leaves pp*1–6* 7–71 *72*

Contents: As A4a but p4 *Printed in Great Britain by* | *John Dickens & Co Ltd* | *Northampton*

White paper covers, black lettering. Front cover: [green key meander pattern between thick red lines] | THE | AGAMEMNON | OF | AESCHYLUS | translated by | LOUIS | MACNEICE | [pattern as above]. Down right-hand side of cover, white lettering on black band: FABER paper covered EDITIONS. Spine lettering: [pattern as front cover] THE AGAMEMNON OF AESCHYLUS · LOUIS MACNEICE (and then white lettering on red band) FABER. Publisher's list on back cover and white lettering on black band as on front cover. White wove paper.

6,000 copies printed. Published September 1967, price 6/-.

A5a   OUT OF THE PICTURE   1937

First edition:
by Louis MacNeice | *a play in two acts* | OUT OF | THE PICTURE | Faber and Faber Limited | 24 Russell Square | London

Collation: 22.5 × 14.5 cm. Π^2 A^8 B–H^8 66 leaves pp*i–iv* 1–4 5 6–8 9–127 *128*

p*i* half-title p*ii* blank p*iii* title-page p*iv* Printed in Great Britain by | R. MacLehose and Company Limited | The University Press Glasgow p*1* To | GRAHAM AND ANNE SHEPARD p*2* blank p*3* Note on first performance p*4* blank p*5* Cast p*6* blank p*7* ACT I p*8* blank pp*9*–*127* text p*128* blank.

Light stone cloth binding, oriental blue lettering stamped down spine: *Out of the Picture by Louis MacNeice Faber & Faber*.
3rd imp. Black dustjacket, black lettering with white shading: OUT OF THE | [white triangle with base to foredge] PICTURE (down foredge with base of letters facing base of triangle) | LOUIS MAC-NEICE | FABER & FABER. Spine lettering: OUT OF THE PICTURE (shaded as on front of jacket) by Louis MacNeice (white lettering). Back of jacket, white, publishers list printed on it. Copies of this imp. have p16 shadowed by double impression.
Cream wove paper, foredge and lower edge leaves untrimmed.

3,040 copies printed. Published June 1937, price 6/-.
2nd imp. October 1937; 3rd imp. October 1946

Notes: First performance p*3*:-
This play is to be produced during the summer of | 1937 by the Group Theatre and Rupert Doone with | music by Benjamin Britten and sets and costumes by | Robert Medley.

A5b   OUT OF THE PICTURE   1938

First American issue:
by Louis MacNeice | *a play in two acts* | OUT OF | THE PICTURE | Harcourt, Brace and Company | New York

Collation: as first edition *but* 22 × 14 cm.

Contents: as first edition

Oxford blue cloth binding; at the top of the spine an Oxford blue label with cream borders at top and bottom: [lettering across] *MacNeice* [lettering down] OUT *of the* | PICTURE | [lettering across] HARCOURT, BRACE | AND COMPANY.
Cream wove paper.
From fragment of dustjacket: cream dustjacket with Oxford blue lettering.
Publisher's note on inside front cover.

520 copies imported from Faber and Faber November 1937, published 24 February 1938, price $1.75.

A6a LETTERS FROM ICELAND 1937

First edition:
W. H. Auden | Louis MacNeice | [short swelled rule intersected by three circles] | LETTERS | FROM ICELAND | [short swelled rule as above] | Faber and Faber | 24 Russell Square | London

Collation: 22 × 14 cm. A^8 B–R^8 136 leaves pp1–8 9–268 269–272

pp1–2 blank p3 half-title p4 blank p5 title-page p6 *Printed in Great Britain by* | R. MacLehose and Company Limited | *The University Press Glasgow* p7 To | GEORGE AUGUSTUS AUDEN p8 blank p9 Preface by WHA and LM p10 blank p11 Contents p12 blank pp13–15 list of illus. and diagrams p16 blank pp17–261 text pp262–268 Appendix pp269–272 blank.
56 half-tone illus.: frontispiece and opp. pp 26, 27, 32, 33, 39, 42, 43, 64, 65, 80, 81, 96, 97, 112, 113, 144, 145, 148, 149, 156, 157, 160, 161, 214, 215, 218, 219, 224, 225. 7 diagrams pp262–268. Foldout map of Iceland opp. p268.

Sea green cloth binding lettering down spine (in signal red) LETTERS FROM ICELAND | (in P.R.U. blue) *W. H. Auden and Louis MacNeice* (then across spine) FABER.
White wove paper.
10,269 copies printed. Published July 1937, price 9/-.
Re-issued July 1941, price 7/6.

Contents:
 LM Contributed prose and poems as follows:
 Chapter III Letter to Graham and Anne Shepard
  „   X Eclogue from Iceland
  „   XII Hetty to Nancy (prose)
  „   XV Iceland
  „   XVII Auden and MacNeice: Their last will and testament
  „   XVII Epilogue for W. H. Auden

A6b LETTERS FROM ICELAND 1937

First American edition:
Letters | FROM ICELAND | BY W. H. AUDEN | AND LOUIS

MACNEICE | RANDOM HOUSE · NEW YORK | [turquoise blue illus of ship steaming past landscape]

Collation: 23 × 15 cm. 1–17⁸ 136 leaves pp*1–16* 17–269 *270–272*

p*1* half-title p*2* blank p*3* title-page p*4* [double thin rule] COPYRIGHT, 1937, BY W. H. AUDEN | MANUFACTURED IN THE U.S.A. p*5* [double thin rule] *To* GEORGE AUGUSTUS AUDEN p*6* blank p*7* Preface p*8* blank p*9* Contents list p*10* blank pp*11–13* list of illus p*14* blank p*15* half-title p*16* blank pp*17–269* text pp*270–272* blank.
Illus. opp. pp 17, 32, 33, 48, 49, 64, 65, 80, 81, 96, 97, 112, 113, 128, 129, 144, 145, 160, 161, 176, 177, 192, 193, 208, 209, 224, 225, 240, 241, 256, 257. 7 diagrams on pp263–269. Map of Iceland on both endpapers.

Beige cloth binding. Front cover, on a cream label, upper-centre: *Letters* | FROM ICELAND | [illus as title page]. Cream label at top of spine: LETTERS | FROM | ICELAND | AUDEN & MACNEICE | Random House | [illus as title-page]. Some copies bound in medium sea grey boards.
White wove paper. Watermark: [top line curved] WARREN'S | OLDE STYLE

3,000 copies printed. Published 23 November 1937, price $3.00.

A6c   LETTERS FROM ICELAND   1967

Second edition:
Title-page as first edition

Collation: 20 × 13 cm. Perfect binding 128 leaves pp*1–6* 7–9 *10* *11* *12–14* 15–253 *254–256*

p*1* half-title p*2* blank p*3* title-page p*4* *Printed in Great Britain by* | *John Dickens & Co Ltd* p*5* To | GEORGE AUGUSTUS AUDEN p*6* blank pp7–9 Foreword by Auden, 1965 p*10* blank p*11* Preface by WHA and LM p*12* blank p*13* Contents p*14* blank pp15–253 text pp*254–255* Map of Iceland p*256* blank.

White paper covers. Front cover: (black) LETTERS | (blue) FROM | (black) ICELAND | [thick signal red line across cover] | (blue) *W.H.* | (black) *Auden &* | (blue) *Louis* | (black) *MacNeice*. French blue band down righthand side with white lettering: FABER paper covered EDITIONS. Lettering down spine: (black) LETTERS FROM ICELAND (blue) W. H. AUDEN & LOUIS MACNEICE (white lettering on red label) FABER. Back cover, blue band with lettering as front cover, with publisher's list continued from inside back cover.

8,000 copies printed. Published December 1967, price 10/6.

Note: Auden's 'Letter to Lord Byron, Part V,' which was Chapter XVI in the first edition, has been dropped; and the last Chapter, 'Auden and MacNeice: Their Last Will and Testament,' which was Chapter XVII, has become XVI.

A6d   LETTERS FROM ICELAND   1969

Second American edition:
LETTERS | FROM | ICELAND | [short swelled rule intersected by three circles] | by W. H. Auden | and Louis MacNeice | [short swelled rule as above] | RANDOM HOUSE · NEW YORK | [publisher's emblem]

Collation: 21.5 × 14.5 cm. A^{16} $B-H^{16}$ 128 leaves pp*1–6* 7–9 *10* 11 12 13 14 15–253 *254–256*

Same contents as English edition 1967 *but* p*2* list of works by Auden; p*4* Manufactured in the United States of America | by the Book Press, Brattleboro, Vermont; p*256* 'About the author' [sic].

Black cloth boards, front and back covers of arctic blue paper. Silver lettering down spine: LETTERS FROM | ICELAND | [across] publisher's emblem | RANDOM | HOUSE | [lettering down] W. H. AUDEN | LOUIS MACNEICE.
White wove paper.

3,000 copies printed. Published 14 April 1969, price $7.50.

Note: same alteration of Chapters as in English edition of 1967.

A7   POEMS 1937   1937

First edition:
BY LOUIS MACNEICE | [ornamental lettering] POEMS | [publisher's emblem] | RANDOM HOUSE : NEW YORK

Collation: 23.5 × 15 cm. $A-G^8$ 56 leaves pp*5–12* 13–115 *116*

p*5* title-page p*6* MANUFACTURED IN THE UNITED STATES OF AMERICA p*7* TO THOSE WHOSE HANDS | ARE FRIENDLY p*8* blank pp*9–10*

B

Contents list p*11* 1. POEMS PUBLISHED IN 1935 p*12* διώκει παῖς ποτανὸν ὄρνιν. ('like a boy who chases a flying bird' Agamemnon, 374) pp*13–115* text p*116* blank.

Black cloth binding, gold lettering. Front cover, lettering in stamped double rule box, at top and bottom of box vertical zig-zag lines: Poems | by | Mac- | Neice. Spine: [lettering in ornamental box as front cover] Poems | by | Mac- | Neice
White wove paper. Watermark: [top-line curved] WARREN'S | OLDE STYLE.

2,000 copies printed. Published 2 December 1937, price $2.50.

Contents:
An eclogue for Christmas—Valediction—Eclogue by a five-barred gate—Morning sun—Turf-stacks—The individualist speaks—Train to Dublin—Cuckoo—The creditor—Perseus—To a communist—Sunday morning—Intimations of mortality—Birmingham—Nature morte—Upon this beach—Snow—Belfast—An April manifesto—A contact—Insidiae—Wolves—August—Aubade—The glacier—Spring voices—Museums—Spring sunshine—Circe—Trapeze—Mayfly—Ode—Glass falling—Trains in the distance—Candle poem—Evening indoors—Song—Homage to clichés—Iceland—June thunder—The heated minutes—Hidden ice—Only let it form—Passage steamer—Sonnet—For services rendered—Leaving Barra—Eclogue from Iceland—The Hebrides—Bagpipe music—Now that the shapes of mist—Epilogue

Notes:
1. Homage to clichés p78 is spelt Homage to clichées in Contents list.
2. Eclogue from Iceland p94 is listed as p96 in Contents list.

A8   THE EARTH COMPELS   1938

First edition:
THE EARTH COMPELS | poems by | LOUIS MACNEICE | Faber and Faber Limited | 24 Russell Square | London

Collation: 22.5×14.5 cm. A^{10} B–D^8 34 leaves pp*i–iv 1–2 3–4 5–6 7–64*

p*i* half-title p*ii* list of works by LM p*iii* title-page p*iv* Printed in Great Britain by | R. MacLehose and Company Limited | The University Press Glasgow p*1* To | NANCY p*2* blank p*3* Contents p*4*

Acknowledgements p5 (δυσέρωτες δὴ φαινόμεθ ὄντες τοῦδ' ὅ τι τοῦτο στίλβει κατα γῆν 'We are plainly sick with love for this glittering something here on earth' Euripides, 'Hippolytus' 193–194) p6 blank pp7–64 text.

Leaf brown cloth binding, gold lettering stamped down spine: *The Earth Compels by Louis MacNeice F & F.*
White wove paper, fore and lower edge leaves untrimmed.

3,640 copies printed. Published April 1938, price 6/-.

Contents:
Carrickfergus—June thunder—The sunlight on the garden—Chess—The heated minutes—Iceland—Solvitur acris hiems—Passage steamer—Circus—Homage to clichés—On those islands—Eclogue from Iceland—Eclogue between the motherless—Leaving Barra—Hidden ice—Taken for granted—Thank you—Books, do not look at me—Only let it form—Now that the shapes of mist—Christmas shopping—Bagpipe music—Rugby football excursion—Epilogue

A9   I CROSSED THE MINCH   1938

First edition:
I CROSSED | THE MINCH | by | LOUIS MACNEICE | *With Eight Drawings* | by NANCY SHARP | LONGMANS, GREEN AND CO. | LONDON * NEW YORK * TORONTO

Collation: 22 × 15 cm. A^8 B–Q^8 R^4 132 leaves pp*i–xii* 1–2 3–248 249–252

pp*i–ii* blank p*iii* half-title p*iv* list of works by LM p*v* title p*vi* publisher's imprint p*vii* To | HECTOR MACIVER p*viii* blank p*ix* Contents p*x* blank p*xi* list of illus. p*xii* blank p*1* PART I VISIT IN APRIL p*2* blank pp3–248 text p*249* blank p*250* MADE AND PRINTED IN GREAT BRITAIN | AT THE BOWERING PRESS, PLYMOUTH pp*251–252* blank.
Illus. opp. pp. 42, 48, 56, 66, 96, 165, 178.

Black cloth binding. Gold lettering across spine: I | CROSSED | THE | MINCH | [swelled rule] | LOUIS | MACNEICE | LONGMANS.
Cream wove paper.

2,000 copies printed. Published April 1938, price 10/6.
Re-issued May 1939, price 5/-.

Note: The following poems are included:
pp33-37   'Dialogue in Stornoway'
p51   'Scottish love song'
pp79-85   'Lord Leverhulme was a grocer's son'
pp157-158   Leaving Barra
pp159-160   Bagpipe music
p175   'The heated minutes climb'
pp245-248   'On those Islands'

A10a   MODERN POETRY   1938

First edition:
MODERN POETRY | A PERSONAL ESSAY | by | LOUIS MACNEICE | OXFORD UNIVERSITY PRESS | 1938

Collation: 19×13.5 cm. A^4 B–Z^4 2A–$2D^4$ 108 leaves pp*i–viii 1 2–205 206–208*

p*i* half-title p*ii* blank p*iii* title-page p*iv* HUMPHREY MILFORD | PUBLISHER TO THE UNIVERSITY | PRINTED IN GREAT BRITAIN p*v* Preface p*vi* blank p*vii* Contents p*viii* blank pp*1–205* text p*206* PRINTED IN | GREAT BRITAIN | AT THE | UNIVERSITY PRESS | OXFORD | BY | JOHN JOHNSON | PRINTER | TO THE | UNIVERSITY pp*207–208* blank.

Signal red cloth binding, gold lettering stamped across spine: MODERN | POETRY | MACNEICE | [O.U.P. crest] | OXFORD.
Cream laid paper.

2,000 copies printed. Published November 1938, price 7/6.

A10b   MODERN POETRY   1968

2nd edition:
MODERN POETRY | A PERSONAL ESSAY | BY | LOUIS MACNEICE | SECOND EDITION | WITH AN INTRODUCTION BY | WALTER ALLEN | OXFORD | AT THE CLARENDON PRESS | 1968

Collation: 19×13.5 cm. A^8 B–N^8 O^4 P^8 116 leaves pp*i–v* vi–xix xx–xxiv 1 2–205 206–208

p*i* half-title p*ii* blank p*iii* title-page p*iv* pub. imprint pp*v–xix* Introduction by Walter Allen p*xx* blank p*xxi* Preface p*xxii* blank p*xxiii* Contents p*xxiv* blank pp*1–205* text pp*206–208* blank.

Oxford blue cloth binding, gold lettering stamped across spine:

[thin gold line] | MODERN | POETRY | MACNEICE | SECOND | EDITION | OUP crest] | OXFORD | [thin gold line]. Cream dustjacket, lettering in emerald green. Front cover: MODERN | POETRY | [pattern: three lines of interlocking diamonds, top and bottom rows in light orange, middle row in green] | *A Personal Essay* | by | *Louis MacNeice* | [pattern as above] | *Second Edition*: *With an introduction by Walter Allen*. Spine lettering: [thin light orange line] | MODERN | POETRY | [light orange diamond shape] | *A Personal Essay* | *by Louis MacNeice* | [thin light orange line, then lettering across spine] | *Second* | *Edition* | [OUP crest in light orange] | OXFORD. Publisher's list on back of jacket. White laid paper.

2,000 copies printed. Published January 1968, price 38/-.

A10c   MODERN POETRY   1969

First American edition:
MODERN POETRY | A PERSONAL ESSAY | by | LOUIS MACNEICE | [publisher's monogram] | HASKELL HOUSE PUBLISHERS LTD. | *Publishers of Scarce Scholarly Books* | NEW YORK, N.Y. 10012 | 1969

Collation: 22.5 × 14 cm. A–E^{16} F^{12} G^{16} (Signatures of the first edition 1938 have been printed) 108 leaves pp*i–viii* 1 2–205 206–208

Contents: As the first edition 1938 *but* p*iv* Printed in the United States of America

Verdigris green cloth binding, gold lettering stamped down spine: MODERN POETRY | A PERSONAL ESSAY LOUIS MACNEICE [then across spine] [publisher's monogram] | HASKELL | HOUSE. Cream wove paper.

No information forthcoming from publisher. Advertised date of publication November 1969, price variably cited as $8.95 and $4.95.

A11   ZOO   1938

First edition:
LOUIS MACNEICE | * | ZOO | ILLUSTRATIONS BY | NANCY SHARP | [pub. device: mermaid] | MICHAEL JOSEPH LTD. | *26, Bloomsbury Street, London, W.C.1.*

Collation: 21 × 15 cm. A^8 B–Q^8 128 leaves pp*1*–4 5 6 7 8 9 *10*–12 13–255 *256*

p*1* half-title p*2* blank p*3* title-page p*4* Set and printed in Great Britain by William Brandon & Son, | Ltd., at the Mayflower Press, Plymouth, in Perpetua type, | twelve point, leaded, on Evensyde Toned Offset Paper made by | John Dickinson, and bound by James Burn p*5* Contents p*6* blank p*7* list of illus. by Nancy Sharp p*8* blank p*9* Preface p*10* blank p*11* first stanza of "Der Panther" by Rilke p*12* illus. pp13–255 text p*256* blank.
Illus. on pp 12, 23, 33, 43, 51, 55, 63, 77, 87, 95, 105, 117, 127, 131, 145, 153, 159, 167, 171, 175, 189, 195, 205, 209, 215, 222, 233, 249, 255.

Eau-de-nil cloth binding. Front cover, lower right-hand corner, silver line-illus of lynx. Silver lettering stamped down spine: LOUIS | MACNEICE | ZOO | [pub. device: mermaid] | MICHAEL | JOSEPH. Yellow endpapers with red line drawing of The Mappin Terraces. Endpapers and cover designed by Nancy Sharp.

2,000 copies printed. Published November 1938, price 10/6.

A12a   AUTUMN JOURNAL   1939

First edition:
AUTUMN JOURNAL | a poem by | LOUIS MACNEICE | Faber and Faber Limited | 24 Russell Square | London

Collation: 22.5 × 14.5 cm. A^8 B–F^8 48 leaves pp*1*–6 7–96
pp*1*–*2* blank p*3* half-title p*4* list of works by LM p*5* title-page p*6* *Printed in Great Britain by* | *Western Printing Services Ltd, Bristol* pp7–8 Note by LM pp9–96 text.

Golden brown cloth binding, gold lettering stamped down spine: Autumn Journal by Louis MacNeice F & F.
White wove paper.
Later imps. reprinted by Latimer Trend & Co Ltd, Whitstable, have pink cloth binding. Dustjacket for 7th imp., light tan with black lettering. Front cover: [thick black line, two thin black lines, and one thinner black line] | Autumn | Journal | [lines as above in inverted sequence] | (on blue band) A Poem | [line sequence as first] | Louis | MacNeice | [line sequence in inverted sequence]. Lettering down spine: [one thick, two thin, and one thinner black line] | Autumn Journal | [inverted line sequence on blue band] | Louis MacNeice Faber. Publisher's list on back of jacket.

5,975 copies printed. Published May 1939, price 6/-.
2nd imp. February 1940; 3rd imp. March 1943; 4th imp. February 1945; 5th imp. January 1946; 6th imp. April 1948; 7th imp. January 1964.

A12b   AUTUMN JOURNAL   1940

First American issue:
AUTUMN JOURNAL | a poem by | LOUIS MACNEICE | [publisher's emblem] | RANDOM HOUSE . NEW YORK | 1940

Collation: 22 × 14 cm. Signatures and pagination as first edition

Contents: As first edition *but* p*vi* PRINTED IN GREAT BRITAIN

Oxford blue cloth binding, gold lettering stamped down spine: Autumn Journal by Louis MacNeice Random House.
White wove paper.

500 copies printed. Published 24 January 1940, price $1.50.

A13   SELECTED POEMS   1940

First edition:
SELECTED POEMS | by | LOUIS MACNEICE | Faber and Faber | 24 Russell Square | London.

Collation: 19.5 × 13 cm. A^8 $B-E^8$ (Gatherings B-E signed M) 40 leaves pp. *1-4* 5 6 *7-80*

p*1* half-title p*2* blank p*3* title p*4* PRINTED IN GREAT BRITAIN BY | WESTERN PRINTING SERVICES LTD., BRISTOL p*5* Select bibliography p*6* blank pp*7-8* Contents pp*9-80* text.

Sky blue paper covered boards, black lettering. Front cover: Selected | Poems | * | Louis MacNeice. Spine lettering: SELECTED POEMS BY LOUIS MACNEICE FABER.
White wove paper.
Later impressions have signal red lettering stamped on binding.

17,430 copies. Published March 1940, price 2/6.
2nd imp. November 1940; 3rd imp. October 1941; 4th imp. February 1943; 5th imp. April 1945.

Contents:
An eclogue for Christmas—Eclogue by a five-barred gate—Sunday morning—Birmingham—Belfast—An April manifesto—Museums—Ode—Carrickfergus—June thunder—The sunlight on

the garden—Eclogue from Iceland—Leaving Barra—Books, do not look at me—Bagpipe music—Autumn journal (Cantos II, IV, VII, IX, XXIV)

A14   THE LAST DITCH   1940

First edition:
THE LAST DITCH | BY | LOUIS MACNEICE | [wood block in black frame 4.5 cm square: landscape with tree in foreground] | THE CUALA PRESS | DUBLIN, IRELAND. | MCMXL

Collation: 21.5 × 15 cm. π^4 A^4 B–F^4 28 leaves pp*i–xvi* *1* 2–33 *34–40* pp*i–viii* blank p*ix* title-page p*x* blank p*xi* (in red) Four hundred and fifty copies of this book | have been printed, of which twenty-five are signed by the author and numbered 1 to 25 p*xii* blank p*xiii* (in red) To Eleanor Clark (p) p*xiv* blank p*xv* Contents p*xvi* blank pp*1–34* (in red) Here ends "The Last Ditch" by Louis | MacNeice. Four hundred and fifty | copies of this book have been printed | and published by The Cuala Press, 133 | Lower Baggot Street, Dublin, Ireland | Finished in the last week of March, nineteen hundred and forty. pp*36–40* blank

Cased in middle blue paper-covered boards with wide white cloth spine. Black lettering across front cover: THE LAST DITCH | BY | LOUIS MACNEICE. White label on spine, black lettering up: THE LAST DITCH · BY LOUIS MACNEICE.
White wove paper, blue cartridge endpapers, all edges untrimmed.

450 copies printed. Published June 1940, price 21/- and 12/6.

Contents:
Prognosis—Dublin—Here in this strange room—Cushendun—The bulletins—Running away from the war—In Sligo the country was soft—Galway—Eastward again—The sky is a lather of stars—Why now it has happened—Meeting point—A toast—London rain—The British Museum Reading Room—Primrose Hill—Departure platform—The old story is true—Suicide—Les sylphides—The gardener—Christina—Three poems apart (for X)

A15   POEMS 1925–1940   1941

First edition:
POEMS | 1925–1940 | BY LOUIS MACNEICE | [publisher's emblem] | RANDOM HOUSE · NEW YORK

Collation: 21 × 14 cm. 1–20⁸ 21⁴ 22⁸ 172 leaves pp*1–2* i–xiv *1–2* 3–326 *327–328*

pp*1–2* blank p*i* half-title p*ii* blank p*iii* title-page p*iv* imprint p*v* Acknowledgments p*vi* blank pvii–xii Contents list pxiii–xiv Foreword p*1* 1 | EARLY POEMS: 1925–1929 p*2* blank pp3–322 text pp323–326 Index of first lines pp*327–328* blank.

Oxford blue cloth binding, silver lettering stamped down spine: [silver line down right-hand side of spine, 6 cm., then across] | POEMS | 1925–1940 | MACNEICE | [silver line across spine then down left-hand side, 11 cm.] | [parallel to line] RANDOM HOUSE.
White wove paper, top edge of leaves are red.
Canary yellow dustjacket with maroon borders along top and bottom. Front cover: [black lettering] LOUIS MACNEICE | POEMS 1925–1940 | [maroon slanted lettering] *The collected poetry of one of the leaders among* | *England's younger generation of poets.* | [publisher's emblem in black] | A RANDOM HOUSE BOOK. Spine: POEMS | [maroon lettering] 1925–1940 | [black lettering] MACNEICE | [publisher's emblem in maroon] | [black lettering] RANDOM | HOUSE. Publisher's list on back of jacket.

2,005 copies printed. Published 17 February 1941, price $2.50.

Contents:
Trains in the distance—Glass falling—The creditor—Kosmos—Poussin—Evening indoors—Happy families—Peripeteia—The court historian—A classical education—Sailor's funeral—River in spate—Candle poem—Trapeze—Spring sunshine—Cradle song for Miriam—Mayfly—Belfast—Birmingham—Turf stacks—Upon this beach—Circe—Spring voices—Museums—Contact—Nature morte—To a communist—Ego—Sunday morning—August—The glacier—Perseus—April—Morning sun—Cuckoo—Train to Dublin—Intimations of mortality—Wolves—Aubade—Snow—Eclogue for Christmas—Eclogue by a five-barred gate—Eclogue from Iceland—Eclogue between the motherless—Valediction—Ode—Homage to clichés—Letter to Graham and Anna—Life of Lord Leverhulme—The Hebrides—The oracle—The daily news—Riding in cars—Hymn of the collectors—War heroes—Pindar is dead—Les neiges d'antan—Empty shoes—Announcer's song—Venus's speech—The jingles of the morning—Auctioneer's speech—Finale—Carrickfergus—Passage steamer—Nocturne—Iceland—Epilogue to Iceland—Solvitur acris hiems—The sunlight on the garden—June thunder—

The heated minutes—Leaving Barra—Sand in the air—Departure platform—Trilogy for X—The brandy glass—Daemonium—Taken for granted—Hidden ice—Chess—Circus—Rugby football excursion—Christmas shopping—Bagpipe music—Autumn journal—Prognosis—Stylite—Entirely—Plant and phantom—The British Museum Reading Room—London rain—Primrose Hill—Men of goodwill—Picture galleries—The coming of war 1. Dublin 2. Cushendun 3. County Sligo 4. Galway 5. Clonmacnois 6. Cushendun again 7. Now it has happened—Meeting point—A toast—Coming from nowhere—Order to view—Novelettes 1. The old story 2. Suicide 3. Les Sylphides 4. The gardener 5. Christina 6. The expert 7. Provence 8. The preacher—The gates of horn—Débâcle—Three thousand miles—Death of an actress—Bar-room matins—Flight of the heart—Refugees—Jehu—Ballades 1. Ballade on an old theme 2. Ballade for Mr. MacLeish 3. Ballade in a bad temper 4. Ballade of dirty linen 5. Ballade for King Canute—O'Connell Bridge—The death-wish—Autobiography—Conversation—The ear—The sense of smell—Evening in Connecticut—Octets 1. Interregnum 2. Barcelona in wartime 3. November afternoon 4. Radio 5. Shopping 6. Business men 7. Night club 8. The lecher 9. Prospect 10. Didymus—Plurality—The undeniable fact—Perdita—The dowser—The return—Cradle song

A16a   THE POETRY OF W. B. YEATS   1941

First edition:

* | LOUIS MACNEICE | THE POETRY OF W. B. YEATS | [swelled rule with five-point stars at each end] | OXFORD UNIVERSITY PRESS | LONDON NEW YORK | TORONTO | 1941

Collation: 22×14 cm. A^8 B–Q^8 128 leaves pp$i$–vi vii–ix x xi xii 1 2–232 233 234–235 236–237 238 242 243–244

pi half-title pii blank piii title-page piv PRINTED IN ENGLAND | AT THE BROADWATER PRESS | WELWYN HERTS pv To E. R. DODDS | AN IRISHMAN, A POET, AND A SCHOLAR, | WHO KNOWS MORE ABOUT IT ALL | THAN I DO pvi And Pan did after Syrinx speed | Not as a nymph, but for a reed. | MARVELL ppvii–ix Preface px blank pxi Contents pxii blank pp1–232 text pp233–235 Notes p236 blank pp237–242 Index pp243–244 blank

Grass green cloth binding, gold lettering stamped across spine: THE | POETRY OF | W. B. YEATS | MACNEICE | OXFORD
White wove paper.

3,500 copies printed. Published February 1941, price 8/6.

A16b   THE POETRY OF W. B. YEATS   1941

First American edition:
Title-page as first edition *but* date has been excluded

> *Collation:* as first edition

> *Contents:* As first edition *but* p*i* blank; p*iv Printed in the United States of America*

> Shell pink cloth binding. Venetian red lettering as first edition. White laid paper.

> 1500 copies printed. Published 3 April 1941, price $2.50.

A16c   THE POETRY OF W. B. YEATS   1967

Second English edition:
The Poetry of | W. B. YEATS | *by* | Louis MacNeice | *with a foreword by* | RICHARD ELLMAN | FABER AND FABER | London

> *Collation:* 19.5 × 13 cm. Perfect binding 104 leaves pp*1–8* 9–11 *12* 13 *14* 15–201 *208*

> pp*1–2* blank p*3* half-title p*4* list of works by LM p*5* title-page p*6 Printed in Great Britain by* | *R. MacLehose and Company Limited* p*7* To | E. R. DODDS | AN IRISHMAN, A POET, AND A SCHOLAR, | WHO KNOWS MORE ABOUT IT ALL | THAN I DO p*8* And Pan did after Syrinx speed | Not as a nymph, but for a reed. | MARVELL pp*9–11* Foreword p*12* blank p*13* Contents p*14* blank pp*15–16* Preface pp17–207 text p*208* blank

> Canary yellow paper front cover: THE | POETRY | OF W. B. | YEATS | [white border] | [lettering on light admiralty grey band] BY LOUIS | MACNEICE | [white border] | [lettering on yellow] With a Foreword | by Richard Ellman. White lettering on deep Brunswick green border down right-hand side: FABER paper covered EDITIONS. Spine lettering: [on yellow] The Poetry of W. B. YEATS [white border] [lettering on grey] Macneice [white border] [white lettering on black band] FABER. Back of cover is white and contains publisher's list, and border lettering as front cover.
> White wove paper.

> 7,000 copies printed. Published June 1967, price 12/6.
> 2nd imp. 1970

A16d   THE POETRY OF W. B. YEATS   1969

Second American edition:
The Poetry of | W. B. YEATS | Louis MacNeice | *with a foreword by* | RICHARD ELLMAN | OXFORD UNIVERSITY PRESS | NEW YORK

Collation: 20 × 13.5 cm. Perfect binding 104 leaves pp*1–8* 9–11 12 13 14 15–207 *208*

Contents: As second English edition *but p6* Printed in the United States of America.

Paper covers. Front cover brilliant green, white lettering: [on mid-Brunswick green area] *The Poetry of* | W. B. YEATS | [then on a brilliant green area] LOUIS MACNEICE | *With a Foreword by* | RICHARD ELLMAN | GB 269 | $1.75. Back of cover is white and contains publisher's description.
White wove paper.

7638 copies printed. Published 13 February 1969, price $1.75.

Notes:
1. Issued as no. 269 in Galaxy Books series.
2. Cover design by Riki.

A17   PLANT AND PHANTOM   1941

First edition:
PLANT AND PHANTOM | poems by | LOUIS MACNEICE | Faber and Faber Limited | 24 Russell Square | London

Collation: 22.5 × 15 cm. A^8 B–E^8 F^4 44 leaves pp*1–8* 9–86 *87–88*

p*1* half-title p*2* list of works by LM p*3* title-page p*4* *Printed in Great Britain by* | *R. MacLehose and Company Limited* | *The University Press Glasgow* p*5* To | ELEANOR CLARK p*6* blank p*7* ein Zwiespalt und Zwitter von Pflanze und von Gespenst | NIETZSCHE p*8* blank pp9–10 Contents p11 Acknowledgments p*12* blank pp13–86 text pp*87–88* blank.

Opaline green cloth binding, gold lettering stamped down spine: *Plant and Phantom by Louis MacNeice F & F.*
Cream wove paper. Untrimmed fore and lower edges.

4,088 copies printed. Published April 1941, price 6/-.

Contents:
Prognosis—Stylite—Conversation—Departure platform—Plant

and phantom—Entirely—The British Museum Reading Room—London rain—Picture galleries—Trilogy for X—Dublin—Cushendun—County Sligo—Galway—Clonmacnois—Cushendun again—Why, now it has happened—Meeting point—A toast—Order to view—The old story—Suicide—Les sylphides—The gardener—Christina—The expert—Provence—The preacher—Débâcle—Exile—Death of an actress—Bar room matins—Flight of the heart—Refugees—Jehu—O'Connell bridge—The deathwish—Autobiography—The ear—Evening in Connecticut—Business men—Night club—Didymus—Plurality—Plain speaking—Perdita—The dowser—The return—Cradle song

A18 MEET THE U.S. ARMY 1943

First edition:
Meet the U.S. Army | Prepared for | The Board of Education | by the | Ministry of Information | London: His Majesty's Stationery Office

Collation: 18.5 × 12 cm. Sewn gathering of 12 leaves pp*1*–5 6–24

p*1* second-half of map of U.S.A. continued from front of inside cover p*2* The text of | this book has been written | for the Board of Education | by | Louis MacNeice p*3* title-page p*4* Contents list pp*5*–24 text.
Eight pages of illus, half-tones, inset between pp12–13.

Signal red paper covers. Front cover has four white stars on the lefthand side of centre, and large white circle as background to the lettering: [white star] | Meet the | [decorative type on white circles] U.S. ARMY | [white star] | [white star] | HIS MAJESTY'S STATIONERY OFFICE 4D. NET | [white star]. Back of cover has publisher's description and note: *Cover printed by Fosh & Cross Ltd. London.*
White wove paper of inferior quality.

Published July 1943, price 4d. H.M.S.O. no longer have records of number of copies printed.

A19a CHRISTOPHER COLUMBUS 1944

First edition:
LOUIS MACNEICE | [swelled rule] | CHRISTOPHER | COLUMBUS | *a radio play* | FABER & FABER

Collation: 22 × 15 cm. A^8 B–E^8 F^6 (2nd leaf signed F2) (gatherings B–F also signed M.C.C.) 46 leaves pp*1*–4 [5]–[92]

p*1* half-title p*2* list of works by LM p*3* title-page p*4* *Printed in Great Britain by* | *R. MacLehose and Company Limited* | *The University Press Glasgow* pp[5]–[6] Cast and note pp[7]–[19] INTRODUCTION | SOME COMMENTS ON RADIO DRAMA p*20* blank pp[21]–[87] text pp[88]–[90] Appendix pp[91]–[92] Notes and addenda.

French blue cloth binding, gold lettering stamped down spine: *Christopher Columbus by Louis MacNeice Faber*
White laid paper. Watermark: [diagram of crown] | A. MILLBURN & CO | BRITISH HAND MADE. Foredge and lower edge leaves untrimmed.
6th imp. Printed in Great Britain by Lowe and Brydone (Printers) Ltd London N.W.10
Dustjacket 5th imp. Blue dustjacket black lettering. Front cover: [red wavy line] | Christopher | Columbus | [red wavy line] | LOUIS MACNEICE. Spine lettering: Christopher Columbus (then red ink) MacNeice (black ink) Faber. Publisher's list on back of jacket.
Dustjacket 6th imp. Yellow dustjacket with same lettering as 5th.

15,500 copies printed. Published March 1944, price 6/-.
2nd imp. April 1944; 3rd imp. November 1949; 4th imp. July 1953; 5th imp. April 1954; 6th imp. March 1961.

Note: First performed BBC Home Service 12 October 1942

A19b   CHRISTOPHER COLUMBUS   1963

2nd edition:
LOUIS MACNEICE | [swelled rule] | CHRISTOPHER | COLUMBUS | *a radio play* | FABER & FABER

Collation: 21 × 14 cm. *A*⁸ B–E⁸ 40 leaves pp*1*–*4* [5]–[80]

p*1* half-title p*2* Faber school editions p*3* title-page p*4* *Printed in Great Britain by* | *Lowe & Brydone (Printers) Ltd* | *London N.W.10* pp[5]–[6] Cast and note on acknowledgments pp[7]–[10] Introduction pp[11]–[77] text p*78* blank pp[79]–[80] Notes.

Olive cloth binding, white lettering on front cover: CHRISTOPHER | COLUMBUS | [swelled rule] | [olive lettering on gold label] FABER | SCHOOL | EDITIONS. White lettering stamped down spine: CHRISTOPHER COLUMBUS Louis MacNeice [white line across spine] | [then across spine] Faber.
White wove paper.

6,050 copies printed. Published 25 September 1963, price 6/6.

A20a SPRINGBOARD 1944

First edition:
LOUIS MACNEICE | [swelled rule] | SPRINGBOARD | *poems* | *1941–1944* | FABER & FABER

Collation: 22.5 × 14.5 cm. A^8 B–C^8 D^4 (gatherings B–D also signed M.S.) 28 leaves pp*1*–*4* 5–54 *55*–*56*

p*1* half-title p*2* list of works by LM p*3* title-page p*4* *Printed in Great Britain by* | *R. MacLehose and Company Limited* | *The University Press Glasgow* pp*5*–*6* Contents and acknowledgments p*7* Note p*8* To Hedli (p) pp*9*–*54* text p*55* Postscript (p) p*56* blank. International orange cloth binding, gold lettering stamped down spine: *Springboard · poems 1941–1944 · Louis MacNeice Faber.* Cream wove paper. Watermark: A. MillBurns & Co | British handmade. Fore and lower edge leaves untrimmed.

7,000 copies printed. Published December 1944, price 6/-.
2nd imp. September 1945

Contents:
Prayer before birth—Precursors—Explorations—Mutations—Brother fire—The trolls—Troll's courtship—Convoy—Sentries—Whit Monday—Swing-song—Bottleneck—Neutrality—The conscript—Nuts in May—The mixer—Nostalgia—Babel—Schizophrene—Alcohol—The libertine—Epitaph for liberal poets—The satirist—This way out—Thyestes—Prayer in mid-passage—Prospect—The springboard—The casualty—The news-reel—The kingdom—Postscript

A20b SPRINGBOARD 1945

First American edition:
POEMS | [thin swelled rule] | *Springboard* | 1941–1944 | [thin swelled rule] | LOUIS MACNEICE | *RANDOM HOUSE NEW YORK*

Collation: 19 × 12.5 cm. A–B^{16} 32 leaves pp*1*–*4* 5–6 *7*–*12* 13–63 *64*

p*1* half-title p*2* blank p*3* title-page p*4* MANUFACTURED IN THE UNITED STATES OF AMERICA pp*5*–*6* Contents list p*7* Note p*8* blank p*9* To Hedli (p) p*10* blank p*11* 1 | [swelled rule] | *Even poisons praise thee* | GEORGE HERBERT p*12* blank pp*13*–*63* text p*64* blank.

Terra cotta cloth binding, gold lettering stamped down spine: LOUIS MACNEICE SPRINGBOARD · *Poems* [in square brackets] *1941* | *1944 RANDOM HOUSE.*
White wove paper.

2,500 copies printed. Published 17 August 1945, price $1.75.

Note: p47 Quotation from Dante is incorrect: Lascio lo fele e vo per dolci pome should be Lascio lo fele e vo per i dolci pomi.

A21a THE DARK TOWER 1947

First edition:
THE | DARK TOWER | *and* | *other radio scripts* | *by* | LOUIS MAC-NEICE | FABER AND FABER LIMITED | 24 Rusesll Square | London

Collation: 21.5 × 14 cm. A^8 B–M^8 N^6 (2nd leaf signed N2) 102 leaves pp*1–8* 9–202 *203–204*

pp*1–2* blank p*3* half-title p*4* list of works by LM p*5* title-page p*6 Printed in Great Britain by* | *R. MacLehose and Company Limited* | *The University Press Glasgow* p*7* Contents p*8* blank pp9–17 General introduction p*18* blank p*19* THE DARK TOWER | *a radio parable play* | To | BENJAMIN BRITTEN p20 Cast pp21–22 Introductory note pp23–66 text p*67* SUNBEAMS IN HIS HAT | *a study of Tchehov* | *as a man* | To | LAURENCE GILLIAM p68 Cast pp69–71 Introductory note p*72* blank pp73–98 text p*99* THE NOSEBAG | *a Russian folk story* | To | FRANCIS DILLON p100 Cast pp101–102 Introductory note pp103–133 text p*134* blank p*135* THE MARCH HARE SAGA | (1) *The March Hare Resigns* | (2) *Salute to all Fools* | To | ESMÉ PERCY pp136–137 Introductory note p138 Cast pp139–163 The march hare resigns p164 Cast pp165–194 Salute to all fools p*195* Notes p*196* blank pp197–202 Notes pp*203–204* blank.

Aircraft grey cloth binding, gold lettering stamped across spine: THE | DARK | TOWER | *& other* | *Broadcast* | *Plays by* | LOUIS MAC- | NEICE | FABER | *and* | FABER. Post-office red dustjacket with black lettering. Front cover: THE DARK | TOWER | and other broadcast plays by | LOUIS | MAC- | NEICE. Spine lettering: THE DARK TOWER | LOUIS | MACNEICE | FABER & | FABER. Publisher's list on back of jacket.
Cream wove paper.

4,000 copies printed. Published May 1947, price 8/6.

Notes: First performances:

The Dark Tower	BBC Home Service			21 January 1946
Sunbeams in his hat	,,	,,	,,	16 July 1944
The Nosebag	,,	,,	,,	13 March 1944
The march hare resigns	,,	,,	,,	29 March 1945
Salute to all fools	,,	,,	,,	1 April 1946

A21b   THE DARK TOWER   1964

First (separate)edition:
THE | DARK TOWER | by | LOUIS MACNEICE | FABER AND FABER LIMITED | 24 Russell Square | London

Collation: 20 × 13 cm. Perfect binding 31 leaves pp*5–8* 9–17 *18–19* 20–66

p*5* half-title p*6* list of works by LM p*7* title-page p*8* *Printed in Great Britain by* | *Latimer Trend & Co Ltd Whitstable* and publisher's note on gummed slip of paper about reprint of General Introduction pp9–17 General Introduction p*18* blank p*19* THE DARK TOWER | *a radio parable play* | To | BENJAMIN BRITTEN p20 Cast pp21–22 Introductory note pp23–66 text.

Paper covers, white background. Front cover: (pink lettering) LOUIS | MACNEICE | (lettering edged with white on black background) THE | DARK | TOWER | (white letters on pink background) FABER. Down right-hand side white lettering on pink band: FABER paper covered EDITIONS. Black lettering down spine: THE DARK TOWER · LOUIS MACNEICE (then white letters on black band) FABER. Back cover: publisher's list and pink band with lettering as front cover.
White wove paper.

10,000 copies printed. Published 12 November 1964, price 5/-.

A22a   HOLES IN THE SKY   1948

First edition:
HOLES IN THE SKY | poems 1944–1947 | by | LOUIS MACNEICE | FABER AND FABER LIMITED | 24 Russell Square | London

Collation: 22.5 × 14.5 cm. A^8 B–D^8 E^4 36 leaves pp*1–10* [11]–[72]

pp*1–2* blank p*3* half-title p*4* list of works by LM p*5* title-page p*6* *Printed in Great Britain by* | *Western Printing Services Limited. Bristol* p*7* Acknowledgments p*8* blank p*9* 'What is truth? says Pilate, . . . (p) p*10* blank p[11] Contents p*12* Note (*on* The Streets of Laredo) pp[13]–[72] text.

Arctic blue cloth binding, silver lettering stamped down spine: HOLES IN THE SKY LOUIS MACNEICE FABER.
White laid paper. Watermark: [diagram of crown] | [in Gothic] Abbey Mills | Greenfield. Top and lower edges untrimmed.

2,650 copies printed. Published 7 May 1948, price 6/-.

Contents:
The streets of Laredo—Hiatus—Corner seat—Aftermath—Twelfth night—Bluebells—Tam cari capitis—The National Gallery—Littoral—The cromlech—Carrick revisited—Slum song—The Strand—Last before America—Western landscape—Under the mountain—No more sea—Godfather—Aubade for infants—The cyclist—Woods—Week-end—Elegy for minor poets—Autolycus—Street scene—Relics—The drunkard—Hands and eyes—Place of a skull—Slow movement—Carol—The Stygian banks—Letter from India

A22b　　　　　　　HOLES IN THE SKY　　　　　　　1949

First American edition:
LOUIS MACNEICE | [olive green swelled rule] | HOLES | IN THE | SKY | Poems 1944–1947 | [publisher's emblem in olive green] | RANDOM HOUSE · NEW YORK

Collation: 22.5 × 15.5 cm A^4 B–E^8 36 leaves *i–viii 1–2 3–61 62–64*

p*i* half-title p*ii* list of books by LM p*iii* title-page p*iv* First published in the United States, January, 1949 imprint and note on previous appearance of some poems p*v* 'What is truth? says Pilate, . . . (p) p*vi* blank p*vii* Contents list p*viii* blank p*1* half-title p*2* Note (on The streets of Laredo) pp*3–61* text pp*62–64* blank.

Boards with terra cotta cloth spine, front and back covers of cream paper with olive green leaf pattern. Gold lettering down spine: HOLES IN THE SKY : *Louis MacNeice* RANDOM HOUSE. On the front cover in bottom left-hand corner is publisher's emblem stamped in gold.
White laid paper.

2,000 copies printed. Published 10 January 1949, price $2.50.

A23a　　　　　COLLECTED POEMS 1925–1948　　　　　1949
First edition:
Collected Poems | 1925–1948 | by | LOUIS MACNEICE | Faber and Faber Limited | 24 Russell Square | London

Collation: 20.5 × 14 cm. A^8 B–T^8 U^4 (gatherings B–U also signed MCP) 156 leaves pp. *1–6 7–310 311–312*

pp*1–2* blank p*3* half-title p*4* list of works by LM p*5* title-page p*6* *Printed in Great Britain by* | *R. MacLehose and Company Limited* | *The University Press Glasgow* p7 Preface p*8* blank pp9–10 To Hedli (p) pp11–16 Contents p*17* 1 | [straight rule] | *1933–1937* p*18* blank pp[19]–[303] text p*304* blank pp[305]–[310] Index of first lines pp*311–312* blank.

'Strong blue' cloth binding, gold lettering across spine: Collected | Poems | *1925–1948* | * | Louis | MacNeice | Faber & Faber.
White wove paper.
Dustjacket 2nd imp., French grey with black lettering. Front cover: Collected | Poems | [red swelled rule] | 1925–1948 | [red swelled rule] Louis | MacNeice. Spine lettering: LOUIS | MAC- | NEICE | [red double rule] | Collect- | ed | Poems | 1925–1948 | [red double rule] | Faber.
Dustjacket 5th imp., light orange, then as above except that white swelled rules replace the red.

12,716 copies printed. Published September 1949, price 12/6.
2nd imp. November 1951; 3rd imp. November 1954; 4th imp. October 1962; 5th imp. January 1965.

Contents:
Eclogue for Christmas—Eclogue by a five-barred gate—Eclogue from Iceland—Eclogue between the motherless—Valediction—Ode—Homage to clichés—Letter to Graham and Anna—The Hebrides—The creditor—Trains in the distance—Genesis—Glass falling—Poussin—Evening indoors—Elephant trunk—River in spate—Candle poems—Nocturne—The lugubrious, salubrious seaside—Happy families—Breaking webs—Mahavveray—Spring sunshine—Cradle song for Miriam—Mayfly—Belfast—Birmingham—Turf-stacks—Upon this beach—Circe—Spring voices—Museums—A contact—Nature morte—To a communist—The individualist speaks—Sunday morning—August—The glacier—Perseus—An April manifesto—Morning sun—Cuckoo—Train to Dublin—Intimations of mortality—Wolves — Aubade — Snow — Carrickfergus — Iceland-Passage steamer—Postscript to Iceland—Sand in the air—Now that the shapes of mist—Hidden ice—The oracle—Riding in cars—War heroes—Pindar is dead—Les neiges d'antan—Empty shoes —The jingles of the morning—Finale—Taken for granted—The brandy glass—The sunlight on the garden—June thunder—The heated minutes—Leaving Barra—Trilogy for X—Chess—Circus—Christmas shopping—Bagpipe music—Autumn journal —Prognosis—Stylite—Entirely—Plant and phantom—The British Museum Reading Room—London rain—Dublin—Cushendun—Sligo and Mayo—Galway—Why, now it has happened—Meeting point—A toast—Order to view—The old story— Les

sylphides—The gardener—Christina—Provence—The preacher—Débâcle—Death of an actress—Bar room matins—Flight of the heart—Refugees—Jehu—The death-wish—Autobiography—Conversation—The ear—Evening in Connecticut—Barcelona in wartime—Business men—Night club—Didymus—Plain speaking—Perdita—The dowser—The return—Cradle song for Eleanor—Prayer before birth—Precursors—Explorations—Mutations—Brother fire—The trolls—Troll's courtship—The revenant—Convoy—Whit Monday—Swing-song—Bottleneck—Neutrality—The conscript—The news-reel—Nuts in May—The mixer—Nostalgia—Babel—Schizophrene—Alcohol—The libertine—Epitaph for liberal poets—The satirist—This way out—Thyestes—Prayer in mid-passage—Prospect—The springboard—When we were children—The streets of Laredo—Hiatus—Corner seat—Aftermath—Twelfth night—Bluebells—Tam cari capitis—The National Gallery—Littoral—The cromlech—Carrick revisited—Slum song—The Strand—Last before America—Under the mountain—No more sea—Godfather—Aubade for infants—The cyclist—Woods—Elegy for minor poets—Autolycus—Street scene—Relics—The drunkard—Hands and eyes—Place of a skull—Slow movement—Carol—Plurality—The casualty—The kingdom—Western landscape—The Stygian banks—Letter from India—The North Sea—Mahabalipuram—The window

A23b   COLLECTED POEMS 1925–1948   1963

First American issue:
Collected Poems | 1925–1948 | by | LOUIS MACNEICE | New York | OXFORD UNIVERSITY PRESS

Collation: As first edition

Contents: As first edition *but* p6 *Printed in Great Britain*
Description as first edition *but* in lettering on spine of binding 'Oxford' replaces 'Faber and Faber'.
869 copies imported. Published 11 April 1963, price $6.00.

A24a   GOETHE'S FAUST   1951

First edition:
[international orange] Goethe's Faust | [black] *Parts I and II* | [thin orange rule] | an abridged version | translated by | LOUIS MAC-NEICE | [pub. monogram in orange] | FABER AND FABER LIMITED | 24 Russell Square | London

Collation: 22.5×15 cm. A^8 B–S^8 T^{10} (2nd leaf signed T*) 154 leaves pp*1–8* 9–306 *307–308*

pp*1–2* blank p*3* half-title p*4* list of works by LM p*5* title-page p*6* Printed in Great Britain by | Latimer Trend & Co Ltd Plymouth p*7* To | my great friend | E. L. STAHL | who went through the German text with me line by | line and without whom I should never have started, | let alone ended, | this translation p*8* blank pp9–10 Introduction p*11* PART I p*12* blank pp13–303 text pp304–306 cuts from text pp*307–308* blank.

Light orange cloth binding, gold lettering stamped across spine: GOETHE'S | FAUST | *transated* | *by Louis* | *MacNeice* | Faber. White wove paper.

3,450 copies printed. Published July 1951, price 15/-.

A24b   GOETHE'S FAUST   1952

First American issue:
[international orange lettering] Goethe's Faust | [black] *Parts I and II* | [thin orange line] | an abridged version | translated by | LOUIS MACNEICE | NEW YORK | OXFORD UNIVERSITY PRESS | 1952

Collation: As first edition

Contents: As first edition *but* p*6* Printed in Great Britain

Description as first edition *but* in lettering on spine of binding 'Oxford' replaces 'Faber'.

1,000 copies imported. Published 28 August 1952, price $4.00.

A24c   GOETHE'S FAUST   1961

First American edition:
Goethe's Faust | *Parts I and II* | [thin line] | an abridged version | translated by | LOUIS MACNEICE | [publisher's emblem] | A Galaxy Book | NEW YORK OXFORD UNIVERSITY PRESS 1960

Collation: 20.5×13.5 cm. Perfect binding 156 leaves pp*1–8* 9–10 11–12 13–306 *307–312*

pp*1–2* blank p*3* half-title p*4* blank p*5* title-page p*6* First published as a Galaxy Book, 1961 p*7* dedication to E. L. Stahl p*8* blank pp9–10 Introduction p*11* PART I p*12* blank pp13–303 text pp304–306 Cuts pp*307–311* Publisher's adverts p*312* blank.

Deep cream paper covers, with full-size dark brown illus. of Mephistopheles in full face, and back view, on front and back covers, respectively. Front cover: [dark brown lettering] Parts I and II | [white lettering] AN UNABRIDGED VERSION TRANSLATED BY | Louis MacNeice | Goethe's FAUST | GB 45 | $1.25. Dark brown lettering down spine: MacNeice Goethe's FAUST [then white lettering across spine] OXFORD | [publisher's emblem] | GB 45. Back cover: [dark brown lettering] POETRY | [white lettering] Goethe's | FAUST | Parts I and II | Translated by LOUIS MACNEICE | [publisher's description and extracts from TLS and Partisan Review reviews] | A GALAXY BOOK · Oxford University Press · New York.
White wove paper.

5,092 copies printed. Published 26 January 1961, price $1.25.
In thirteen subsequent impressions 105,102 copies have been printed.

Notes:
1. Issued as no. 45 in Galaxy Books series.
2. Cover design by Lorraine Blake

A24d GOETHE'S FAUST 1965

Second English impression:
Goethe's Faust | *Parts I and II* | [thin line] | an abridged version | translated by | LOUIS MACNEICE | and | E. L. STAHL | *Taylor Professor of the* | *German Language and Literature* | *in the University of Oxford* | FABER AND FABER LIMITED | 24 Russell Square | London

Collation: 19.5 × 13 cm. Perfect binding. 154 leaves pp*1–8* 9–10 *11–12* 13–306 *307–308*

pp*1–4* blank p*5* half-title p*6* list of works by LM p*7* title-page p*8 Printed in Great Britain by | Latimer Trend & Co Ltd Whitstable* pp9–10 Introduction p*11* PART I p*12* blank pp13–306 text pp*307–308* blank

Paper covers, white background. Front cover: Goethe's | [in international orange ornamental box] FAUST | PARTS I & II | [swelled int. orange rule] | an abridged version translated by | Louis MacNeice | and | E. L. Stahl. Down right-hand side, white lettering on black band: FABER paper covered EDITIONS. Black spine lettering: Goethe's FAUST Parts I and II white lettering on orange background FABER | [orange lettering] LOUIS MACNEICE

and E. L. STAHL. Back cover: publisher's list and black band with lettering as front cover.
White wove paper.

6,075 copies printed. Published 9 December 1965, price 10/6.

A25a   TEN BURNT OFFERINGS   1952

First edition:
TEN | BURNT | OFFERINGS | by | LOUIS MACNEICE | FABER AND FABER | 24 Russell Square | London

Collation: 22.5 × 14.5 cm. A^8 B–F^8 48 leaves pp*1–8* 9–10 *11–12* 13–95 *96*

pp*1–2* blank p*3* half-title p*4* list of works by LM p*5* title-page p*6* *Printed in Great Britain by | R. MacLehose and Company Limited | The University Press Glasgow* p*7* 'Every voyage is a death...' Mayday 1951 p*8* blank p*9* Contents p*10* Acknowledgments p*11* I p*12* blank pp*13–96* text.

Rose pink cloth binding, gold lettering stamped down spine: TEN BURNT OFFERINGS Louis MacNeice Faber.
Cream wove paper.

3,000 copies printed. Published 11 July 1952, price 10/6.

Contents:
Suite for recorders—Aeropagus—Cock o' the north—Didymus—Our sister water—The island—Day of renewal—Day of returning—The death of a cat—Flowers in the interval

Note: p10 'some had already been broadcast' i.e. Suite for recorders, Cock o' the north, Didymus were broadcast on 15 September 1951, the programme repeated 18 November 1951.

A25b   TEN BURNT OFFERINGS   1953

First American issue:
TEN | BURNT | OFFERINGS | by | LOUIS | MACNEICE | New York | OXFORD UNIVERSITY PRESS | 1953

Collation: As first edition

Contents: As first edition *but* p*6 Printed in Great Britain*

Description as first edition *but* in lettering on spine of binding 'Oxford' replaces 'Faber'.

Publisher has no records about this book. Published 26 February 1953, price $2.50.

A26a   THE PENNY THAT ROLLED AWAY   1954

First edition:
LOUIS MACNEICE | [in a circle around a drawing of a falling infant] THE PENNY THAT ROLLED AWAY 1954 | *ILLUS-TRATIONS BY* | MARVIN BILECK | G. P. PUTNAM'S SON NEW YORK N.Y.

Collation: 17 × 16 cm. $A^6 B^8 C^6$ 20 leaves pp1–6 7–37 38–40

p1 half-title p2 blank p3 title-page p4 MANUFACTURED IN THE UNITED STATES BY THE POLYGRAPHIC COMPANY OF AMERICA, INC. p5 half-title p6 part of a drawing pp7–38 text p39 ABOUT THE AUTHOR p40 blank

Cardboard covers with pattern of one cent coins in rows in which front and back of coin alternate; coins are pink with black lettering and numerals, separated by black leaf pattern. Spine reads down in black: MACNEICE THE PENNY THAT ROLLED AWAY *Putnam*.
White wove paper.

Publisher has no records about this book. Published 26 February 1954, price $2.25.

A26b   THE SIXPENCE THAT ROLLED AWAY   1956

First English edition:
The Sixpence | that Rolled Away | by | LOUIS MACNEICE | *illustrated by* | EDWARD BAWDEN | [black and white illus. of upside-down figure] | FABER AND FABER | 24 Russell Square | London

Collation: 21 × 15.5 cm. A–C^4 12 leaves pp1–6 [7]–[24]

pp1–2 blank p3 half-title p4 blank p5 title-page p6 imprint and instructions to binder about the positioning of colour plates: PRINTED IN GREAT BRITAIN BY | LATIMER, TREND AND CO LTD PLYMOUTH pp[7]–[24] text.

Colour plates opp. pp. [9], [12], [16], [20] and [24].

Cardboard packed boards with arctic blue paper covering and Light Brunswick green cloth spine. Front cover: [left-hand side: brown, yellow and white illus. of cuckoo clock]: [right-hand side: picture of cuckoo with text underneath] | The | Sixpence |

that | Rolled | Away | by Louis | MacNeice | Illustrated by | Edward Bawden. Gold lettering stamped up spine: THE SIXPENCE THAT ROLLED AWAY MACNEICE. On the middle of the back cover is the same illus. as the title-page.
White wove paper.
4,000 copies printed. Published 23 November 1956, price 10/6.

Note: For the English edition, the title and names in the story have been changed from their equivalents in the American edition.

A27   THE OTHER WING   1954

First edition:
The Other Wing | *by* | LOUIS MACNEICE | *illustrated by* | MICHAEL AYRTON | [illus. of display in museum case: 6 × 4 cm.] | FABER AND FABER | 24 Russell Square London WC1

Collation: 21.5 × 14 cm. Sewn gathering of 2 leaves pp*1–4*

p*1* title-page p*2* coloured litho illus. of Athena emerging from the head of Zeus p*3* text p*4* text and imprint: Printed in Great Britain by Jesse Broad & Co. Ltd, Manchester.

French blue paper covers, black lettering. Front cover: *Ariel Poem* | [two swelled rules intersected by rose with two stems] | THE OTHER | WING | *by* | LOUIS MACNEICE | *illustrated by* | MICHAEL AYRTON | [printer's device as above] | FABER AND FABER. On the back of inside cover two line drawings: on left-hand side madonna and child in frame: on right-hand side, mummy in coffin. On the back of the cover is a publisher's list of the Ariel series within three-lined box, with stars at each corner.
White wove paper.

5,130 copies printed. Published 1 November 1954, price 2/-.

A28   AUTUMN SEQUEL   1954

First edition:
AUTUMN SEQUEL | [printer's device: swelled rule intersected by circle] | *A Rhetorical Poem in XXVI Cantos* | *by* | LOUIS MACNEICE | FABER AND FABER LIMITED | 24 Russell Square, | London

Collation: 22.5 × 15 cm. A^8 B–I^8 K^{10} (2nd leaf signed K*) (gatherings B–K also signed AS) 82 leaves pp*1–6 7 8–10 11–163 164*

pp*1–2* blank p*3* half-title p*4* list of works by LM p*5* title-page p*6* Printed in England by | *Western Printing Services Limited, Bristol* p7 Prefatory note p8 blank p9 *Do I contradict myself? | Very well then I contradict myself...* | WALT WHITMAN p*10* blank pp11–163 text p*164* blank.

Dark violet cloth binding, gold lettering stamped down spine: *Autumn Sequel by Louis MacNeice* (then across spine) *Faber*. Pale blue dustjacket with black and red lettering: (black) AUTUMN | SEQUEL | (red) | *A Rhetorical Poem* | *in XXVI Cantos* | *by* | (black) LOUIS | MACNEICE | [swelled rule] | (red) *FABER*. Red and gold lettering across spine: (black) Autumn | Sequel | * | Louis | MacNeice | [swelled rule] | (then down spine in red) AUTUMN SEQUEL | LOUIS MACNEICE | [swelled rule] | (then down spine in black) Faber | and | Faber. Publisher's list on back of jacket.
White wove paper.

4,000 copies printed. Published 12 November 1954, price 12/6.

Note: Prefatory note p7 'bulk of it was broadcast by BBC in Summer 1954' i.e. six programmes 45 minutes each, broadcast in May, excepting Cantos 4, 6, 9, 12, 13, 19, 21 and 23.

A29a   VISITATIONS   1957

First edition:
VISITATIONS | by | LOUIS MACNEICE | FABER AND FABER | 24 Russell Square | London

Collation: 22 × 14.5 cm. A^8 $B-D^8$ 32 leaves pp*1–8* 9 *10–12* 13–60 *61–64*

pp*1–2* blank p*3* half-title p*4* list of works by LM p*5* title-page p*6 Printed in Great Britain | by The Bowering Press Plymouth* p7 To Hedli (p) p*8* blank p9 Acknowledgments p*10* blank p*11* Contents p*12* blank p13–60 text pp*61–64* blank.

'Strong blue' cloth binding, gold lettering stamped down spine: VISITATIONS by Louis MacNeice F & F. Pale blue dustjacket with black lettering. Front cover: Visitations | [printer's device in red: decorative rule] | *poems by* | LOUIS MACNEICE. Black spine lettering: VISITATIONS (red) by (black) LOUIS MACNEICE (red) Faber. Publisher's list on back of jacket.
White wove paper.

4,000 copies printed. Published 10 May 1957, price 10/6.
2nd imp. 1959 printed by Bradford and Dickens, Drayton House London W.C.1.

Contents:
To the public—To posterity—April fool—Dreams in middle age—Sailing orders—Donegal tryptich—The left-behind—The back-again—The gone-tomorrow—The once-in-passing—The here-and-never—Wessex guidebook—The rest house—Beni Hasan—Return to Lahore—Visit to Rouen—Time for a smoke—Jigsaws: i–v—Easter returns—The other wing—The burnt bridge—The tree of guilt—House on a cliff—Figure of eight—Death of an old lady—Visitations: i–vii

Note: Summer choice 1957 Poetry Book Society *see* Poetry Book Society Bulletin May 1957.

A29b   VISITATIONS   1958

First American issue:
VISITATIONS | by | LOUIS MACNEICE | New York | OXFORD UNIVERSITY PRESS | 1958

Collation: As first edition

Contents: As first edition *but* p6 Printed in Great Britain

Description as first edition *but* lettering on spine of binding and dustjacket varies: 'Oxford' replaces 'F & F' on binding: 'Oxford' replaces 'Faber' on dustjacket.

Publisher has no record of number of copies imported. Published 22 May 1958, price $3.00, later advertised as $1.70.

A30a   EIGHTY-FIVE POEMS   1959

First edition:
LOUIS MACNEICE | * | *Eighty-Five Poems* | Selected by the Author | FABER AND FABER | 24 Russell Square | London

Collation: 19 × 13 cm. A^8 B–H^8 (gatherings B–H also signed EFP) 64 leaves pp*1*–4 5–7 *8* 9–11 *12* 13–128

p*1* half-title p*2* list of works by LM p*3* title-page p*4* *Printed in Great Britain by* | *Western Printing Services Limited Bristol* pp5–6 To Hedli (p) p7 Foreword p*8* blank pp9–11 Contents p*12* blank pp13–128 text.

Maroon cloth binding, white lettering stamped down spine: *Eighty-Five Poems* | [vertical white line] | LOUIS MACNEICE | [vertical white line] | *Faber*. Admiralty grey dustjacket, leaf

brown lettering between grass green vertical lines. Front cover: Louis MacNeice | [grass green swelled rule] | Eighty-Five | POEMS | [green swelled rule] | selected | by the author. Lettering down spine: Eighty-Five POEMS Louis MacNeice [thin green swelled rule] Faber. Publisher's list on back of jacket.
Cream wove paper.

3,000 copies printed. Published 13 February 1959, price 10/6.

Contents:
Littoral—The creditor—Nostalgia—Conversation—Precursors—Snow—The return—The muse—The riddle—Autobiography—Woods—Wessex Guidebook—The cyclist—Candles—Perseus—Hands and eyes—The window—Carrickfergus—The gardener—Dublin—Slum song—Turf stacks—Last before America—The left-behind—The back-again—The gone-tomorrow—Train to Dublin—The Strand—Death of an old lady—Homage to clichés—Spring voices—Sunday morning—August—Museums—Nature morte—Wolves—An eclogue for Christmas—The individualist speaks—Iceland—Bagpipe music—Entered in the Minutes [i–iv]—The British Museum Reading Room—London rain—Street scene—Relics—Les sylphides—The libertine—Christina—Figure of eight—House on a cliff—Slow movement—June thunder—First light—Leaving Barra—The sunlight on the garden—The kingdom—Order to view—Meeting point—A toast—The merman—The revenant—Prognosis—Thyestes—Bar room matins—Death of an actress—Evening in Connecticut—Nuts in May—Brother fire—The streets of Laredo—Convoy—The springboard—The casualty—Rites of war—Bluebells—Mahabalipuram—Didymus—The other wing—Easter returns—Prayer in mid-passage—The brandy glass—Sailing orders—Prayer before birth—The dowser—Day of returning

A30b   EIGHTY-FIVE POEMS   1961

First American issue:
LOUIS MACNEICE | * | Eighty-Five Poems | Selected by the Author | New York | OXFORD UNIVERSITY PRESS

Collation: As first edition

Contents: As first edition *but* p4 *Printed in Great Britain*

Description as first edition *but* in lettering on spine of binding and dustjacket 'Oxford' replaces 'Faber'.

625 copies imported. Published 4 May 1961, price $3.25.

A31a SOLSTICES 1961
First edition:
SOLSTICES | by | LOUIS MACNEICE | FABER AND FABER LIMITED | 24 Russell Square | London

Collation: 22×14.5 cm. A^8 B–E^8 40 leaves pp*1–8* [9]–[10] *11–12* [*13*]–[*78*] *79–80*

pp*1–2* blank p*3* half-title p*4* list of works by LM p*5* title-page p*6 Printed in Great Britain | at the Bowering Press Plymouth* p*7* . . . age iam meorum | finis amorum . . . p*8* blank pp[9]–[10] Contents p*11* Note by LM p*12* blank pp[*13*]–[*78*] text pp*79–80* blank.

Maroon cloth binding, gold lettering stamped down spine: SOLSTICES *by Louis MacNeice Faber*. Eau-de-nil dustjacket with crimson bands down each long side, and two crimson bands in middle of cover, one at top and one at bottom, ending in concaves. Between crimson bands on left side, lettering up: SOLSTICES. Between crimson bands on right hand side, lettering down: SOLSTICES. Between concave-end bands in centre of cover: LOUIS | MAC- | NEICE | POEMS. Lettering down spine: SOLSTICES · LOUIS MACNEICE FABER. Publisher's list on back of jacket. White wove paper.

3,200 copies printed. Published 10 March 1961, price 12/6.

Contents:
Apple blossom—Invocation—The riddle—Notes for a biography—The slow starter—Il piccolo rifiuto—The messiah—The Atlantic tunnel—Homage to Wren—Rites of war—Jericho—Yours next—on the Venerable Bede—on the Grettir saga—on the Njal saga—on the four masters—Darts—Shove halfpenny—Vingt-et-un—Crossword puzzles—Idle talk—Country weekend Dandelions—Cats—Corncrakes—The sea—Sleeping winds [i–iv]—The park—The lake in the park—Dogs in the park—Sunday in the park—Windowscape—Solstice—Indian village—Jungle clearance Ceylon—Half truth from Capetown—Solitary travel—Old masters abroad—Icebergs—Vistas—Variation on Heraclitus—Reflections—Hold-up—Restaurant car—The wiper—The wall—The snow man—The truisms—The blasphemies—Bad dream—Good dream—Selva oscurae—All over again

Note: Spring 1961 recommendation of the Poetry Book Society *see* Poetry Book Society Bulletin February 1961.

A31b   SOLSTICES   1961

First American issue:
SOLSTICES | by |LOUIS MACNEICE | New York | OXFORD UNIVERSITY PRESS | 1961

Collation: As first edition

Contents: As first edition *but* p6 *Printed in Great Britain*

Description as first edition *but* in lettering on spine of binding and dustjacket 'Oxford' replaces 'Faber'.

Publisher has no record of number of copies imported. Published 24 August 1961, price $3.50.

A32a   THE BURNING PERCH   1963

First edition:
THE | BURNING PERCH | [printer's device: two parallel lines, the lower shaded, intersected by three diamonds] | Louis MacNeice | FABER AND FABER | 24 Russell Square | London

Collation: 22 × 14.5 A^8 B–C^8 D^6 30 leaves pp*1–8* 9–58 *59–60*

pp*1–2* blank p*3* half-title p*4* list of works by LM p*5* title-page p*6* *Printed in Great Britain by* | *The Bowering Press Plymouth* p*7* To Mary (p) p*8* blank pp9–10 Contents pp11–58 text pp*59–60* blank.

Maroon cloth binding, gold lettering down spine: THE BURNING PERCH · LOUIS MACNEICE . Faber and Faber. Salmon pink dustjacket, black lettering: THE | BURNING | PERCH | (signal red) LOUIS | MAC- | NEICE. On right hand side of cover red wavy line for three quarters of length. Spine lettering: THE BURNING PERCH (signal red) LOUIS MACNEICE (black) FABER. Publisher's list on back of jacket. White wove paper.

7,060 copies printed. Published 13 September 1963, price 12/6.

Contents:
Soap suds—Déjà vu—Round the corner—The suicide—Perspectives—Château Jackson—Pet shop—Flower shop—In lieu—The taxis—The grey ones—After the crash—Spring cleaning—Another cold May—The pale panther—Rechauffé—Ravenna—Constant—October in Bloomsbury—New Jerusalem—Charon—The introduction—Birthright—Children's games—Tree party—Sports page—The habits—Greyness is all—As in their time—

This is the life—Budgie—Memoranda to Horace—Star-gazer—Goodbye to London—Off the peg—Coda

Note: Autumn choice of the Poetry Book Society *see* Poetry Book Society Bulletin September 1963.

A32b   THE BURNING PERCH   1963

First American issue:
THE | BURNING PERCH | [printer's device: two parallel lines, the lower shaded, intersected by three diamonds] | Louis MacNeice | New York | OXFORD UNIVERSITY PRESS | 1963

Collation: As first edition

Contents: As first edition *but p6 Printed in Great Britain*

Description as first edition *but* in lettering on spine of binding 'Oxford' replaces 'Faber and Faber'.

780 copies imported. Published 17 October 1963, price $3.75.

A33 THE MAD ISLANDS AND THE ADMINISTRATOR 1964
First edition:
THE MAD ISLANDS | and | THE ADMINISTRATOR | *Two radio plays* | by | LOUIS MACNEICE | FABER AND FABER | 24 Russell Square | London

Collation: 22 × 14 cm. A^8 $B-G^8$ 56 leaves pp*1*–*4* 5 6 *7*–9 *10*–*12* 13–69 *70*–*72* 73–112

p*1* half-title p*2* list of works by LM p*3* title-page p*4* *Printed in Great Britain | by The Bowering Press Plymouth* p*5* Contents p*6* blank pp7–9 Introduction p*10* blank p*11* THE MAD ISLANDS p*12* blank p13 Main characters p14 Cast and details of 1st performance pp15–69 text p*70* blank p*71* THE ADMINISTRATOR p*72* blank p73 Main characters p74 Cast and details of 1st performance pp75–112 text.

Dark violet cloth binding, gold lettering stamped down spine: *The Mad Islands and The Administrator* by Louis MacNeice (then across spine) Faber. White dustjacket with two light orange segments across front cover, lettering in black: LOUIS | MACNEICE (on white) | The | Mad Islands (on light orange) | & (on white) | The | Administrator (on light orange). Spine lettering: LOUIS

MACNEICE (on white) The Mad Islands (on light orange) & (on white) The Administrator (and then across spine on light orange) Faber. Publisher's list on back of jacket.
White wove paper.

2,000 copies printed. Published 13 March 1964, price 18/-.
390 copies were imported into the U.S.A. by Oxford University Press, New York, and issued on 16 April 1964, price $4.25.

Notes: First performances:

The Mad Islands	BBC Third Programme	4 April 1962
The Administrator	,, ,, ,,	10 March 1961

A34a   ASTROLOGY   1964

First edition:
Astrology Louis MacNeice

Collation: 25×17 cm. $1-22^8$ 176 leaves pp1–7 8–301 302–323 324–326 327–343 344–351 352

pp1–2 blank p3 half-title p4 SOL | [blue woodblock: man driving chariot] | Editorial adviser Donald Berwick | Editor Douglas Hill | Editorial assistants Joanna Evans | Diana Souhami | Art editor Valerie Zweig | Art assistants Behram Kapadia | Michael King | Research A. F. Walker | Aldus Books, London | in association with W. H. Allen London p5 title-page p6 blue line diagram and imprint: Printed in Holland by N. V. Drukkerij Senefelder, Amsterdam p7 Contents list pp8–288 text p289 Appendices pp290–297 Appendix I Elements of the Horoscope pp298–301 Appendix 3 [sic] National horoscopes pp302–326 Appendix 2 Tables of Sidereal time pp327–343 Ephemerides of the planets pp344–349 Index pp350–351 Acknowledgments p352 blank

Black cloth binding, Middle of front cover astrological circle stamped in gold. Gold lettering stamped down spine: Louis MacNeice Astrology Aldus. White dustjacket, front cover: Astrology | Louis MacNeice | [circular photograph of sky at night: across diameter 5 of the 12 signs of Zodiac]. Lettering across spine: Astrology | MacNeice | [smaller copy of photograph on front cover in elongated oval shape: one of remaining Zodiac signs across diameter]. Back of jacket: [photograph of one of the stages involved in casting a horoscope] | [remaining six signs of Zodiac] | [a note on photographs used on jacket].
White wove paper, blue pendpapers.

IMPRESSION

OF LAST WEEK'S MEETING OF THE POETRY SOCIETY FOLLOWING SOME OF THE SUGGESTIONS PUT FORWARD WITH APOLOGIES TO MISS STEIN AND MR. CUMMINGS.

[i] said
sAid
(said)——!
gaS——! works
" Works "
said
GAs(wor)Ks
and ?
; mind you
I said mind YOU
(you) ? I Said
  [Works]
    a flOWer.
what ?
  WHat ?
    What ? !
i (s)aiD
don't inteRRupt !
—I said (don't)
A FLowER
and
i said
gas-
  works
Beauty
OH ! beauty ! beauty ! beauty !
aNd (math)ematicS
Don't
i sai(d)
forget

forget
I said
  forget
OH dear oh d(E)ar !
mathematics
and gAs-works
Flowers floWers
mild mathematical
paTTerns
erratic
(oF)
gAs-works (& !)
flowers
Why ?
  Why ?
    Why ?
WHy not flOral gAs-works ? !
Intellect ?
Don'T
i said
just ReflEct
gAs-works
—or ! ice-cream
bUt Why
, , ? Why WHy ?
I said
(said !)
Does no one think of anything better to say ?
                      UNDERGRADUETTE.
                                  L.M.H.

To the Editor. DEAR SIR,—I was moved to the following last Monday evening :—

PARADISE LOST
(VILLANELLE)

[. . . " *cuncta prospectabam loca, sicubi forte conterminis in hortulis candens repperirem rosarium.*"—APULEIUS.]

CAUGHT in Apollo's blended dream
  On the dim marge of Poesy
    My rose-red lips unlock to scream.

My horticultural mind did teem
With roses once and rosemary
Caught in Apollo's blended dream.

Now an unorthodox regime
Has whelmed my soul in lethargy,
My rose-red lips unlock to scream.

The sinister tall gas-works seem
To vitiate my destiny
Caught in Apollo's blended dream.

Plenty is plethora they deem
And advocate phlebotomy—
My rose-red lips unlock to scream—

And quantities of bad ice-cream.
Ah God ! my world is fall'n from me.
Caught in Apollo's blended dream
My rose-red lips unlock to scream.
                JOHN BOGUS ROSIFER,
                            Keble College.

Sir Galahad, February 1929 (B33)

were yelling homeward and a coal-cart was rounding the corner. Each morning, it was certain, the milkman would clatter his lids outside the door. There would never be any escape that way from the arid desolation of the room. However, he had asked to see it, he must therefore promise to consider and write about it. So he leant against the faded wallpaper, and scribbled out his name and address. The little landlady peered over it suspiciously, pushing aside a damp, grey wisp of her hair.

A narrow dark rather aristocratic street received him. Tired of his inquiries he decided it was the last one he would search. Very straight and sombre its houses uprose, as in an etching, keeping out the sun. One or two figures slunk past unobtrusively, as though submitting to its dankness, along the walls. Before long he, too, felt the past weighing on him in its deserted balconies, and its tall, draped windows, with their funereal bowls of flowers. He knocked at one of the doors, and it opened, almost stealthily, admitting him to a little shadowy hall, where the polished corners of furniture glimmered in the darkness. An old woman was bending towards him, not resentfully, like the others, but with an aged fragile kind of grace. Everywhere was the sweet indefinable odour of the house carrying back the mind. They crossed to a room at the other end, of the shadowy hall, and the old woman knocked softly that they might enter. It was quiet and pale inside, lit by a large low window into the garden. At a table against the window a girl was seated writing. The old woman stood aside for him to look in, and the girl in the chair turned half-round, uncertain whether to continue. Dark and smiling her face was uplifted against the pale light. Its warm, carven immobility excited him so that he had seen little of the room, when the old woman beckoned him upstairs. She climbed with slow, accustomed steps, resting heavily at each landing. He followed her, thinking of the smiling silhouette of the girl, and breathing in the quaint timeless odour of the house. Once at a corner, a pier-glass, for a half-conscious instant, flashed back his identity. When they had looked at the bedroom the old woman insisted, although he had made his choice, on showing him two others. He listened to her thin quavering voice, as it ran on, in a kind of dazed pleasure. At present he scarcely cared if he were late. It was the house and the girl's uplifted face which had changed him. His life there in the quiet pale room would be very agreeable, he thought. Its glamour made all his history, spread out before him, vibrate with a new significance.

Saying good-bye to the old landlady he stepped down into the street. Something of his happiness still clung to him as he walked away. But the charm was decaying, and soon it began to flake up and fall from him. Try as he might he could not preserve it from the strangers who brushed against him, or from the tired crescendoes of the traffic. The harsh frightening confusion of the city was pressing round him again. It was snatching up his mood like bits of newspaper in the wind; and before long he ceased to resist it. He remembered, with cynical sadness, the sudden moments of exhilaration which passed over him when he was a boy, going back to school; and how they always disappeared again, as quickly and inexplicably as they had come.

J. R. V. COLLIN.

※ ※ ※

SAUL

Splendour topples over the rim
And is soon spent;
Saul glooms within the tent;
Blooms within the fender fall.
For coal and soul in the last event
Have their epitaphs in charcoal.

Charred his soul, the heavy canvas
Lowers upon him doomfully;
The fire upon the hearth is out,
The stars have fallen out of the sky,
Saul is tired, tired to death of royalty.

Royalty's flaunting tongues
Of red bitter flame
Muttered and ranted poisonously,
Rancorously conspired,
But now deflowered of pollen, deprived of life,

A smattering of ashes, gone their breath,
Saul the king is tired of the orb he holds
And the orb he lives on and tired
Literally to death.

. . . . . .

Your business, sir? I have come to see the king
You may not see him now. I must; it is pressing
You cannot. Why, is the king dressing?
No. Is he holding council? No. Then what
I beg your pardon, sir, but it is not
Any manner of use your guessing—
The king is dead within.

Sharp
The wind combs the grasses;
A young man passes
Carrying something—
A harp, I think. ANON

Sir Galahad, May 1929 (B34)

Re-issued by Spring Books 1965. Differences: p4 illus. of SOL in black and at bottom of page: Spring Books London p6 illus in black.
Black cloth binding, astrological circle on cover in slightly higher position. Gold lettering up spine: Louis MacNeice Astrology (then at bottom of spine and across) Spring | Books

25,500 copies printed in total English editions. Published 14 September 1964, price 63/-.

Notes:
1. Appendix 2 is incorrectly numbered 3; Appendix 3 is incorrectly numbered 2.
2. The pagination for the Acknowledgments does not correspond with that in the Contents List.
3. Also published in France by Tallandier with 12,000 copies; in Germany by Ullstein, 10,000 copies; in Italy by Rizzoli, 5,000 copies; in Spain by Cara lt., 4,000 copies.

A34b ASTROLOGY 1964

First American edition:
Astrology Louis MacNeice | [blue woodblock: man driving chariot] | Doubleday & Company Inc., | Garden City, New York

Collation: As first edition

Contents: As first edition *but* p4 blank; p6 Library of Congress number added

Black cloth binding, Front cover has astrological circle stamped off-centre right. Gold lettering stamped down spine: MacNeice Astrology Doubleday. Shaded blue dustjacket on front cover and spine, back cover white. Front cover: [within yellow ruled box publisher's description] | [white lettering] LOUIS MACNEICE | [yellow lettering] ASTROLOGY | [illus. in circular form of signs of Zodiac, in centre of which is a goat]. Spine: [yellow lettierng] *ASTROLOGY* [white lettering] LOUIS | MACNEICE [then across bottom of spine] DOUBLEDAY. Back cover: [blue] *ASTROLOGY* | [black] LOUIS MACNEICE | [illus. in black as front cover] [within blue ruled box a note about the author].
White wove paper, blue endpapers.

20,000 copies printed. Published November 1964, price $9.95.
11,000 copies in 2nd impression July 1967, price $5.95.

25,000 copies in three more impressions during 1969. 10,000 copies in 6th impression February 1970, price $6.95.

Notes:
1. Errors in numbering of Appendices 2 and 3, and pagination of Acknowledgments, as first edition.
2. Jacket designed by Don Moss, printed in Yugoslavia.

A35   SELECTED POEMS   1964

First edition:
LOUIS MACNEICE | *Selected Poems* | *Selected* | *and introduced by* | W. H. AUDEN | FABER AND FABER | 24 Russell Square | London

Collation: 18.5 × 12 cm. Perfect binding 80 leaves pp*1*–4 5–160

p*1* half-title p*2* list of works by LM p*3* title-page p*4* *Printed in Great Britain by* | *R. MacLehose and Company Limited* | *The University Press Glasgow* pp5–7 Contents p8 Note on arrangement of poems pp9–10 Introduction pp11–160 text.

White paper covers. Front cover: (black lettering) Selected | Poems of | Louis | MacNeice | [thick sea green band] | (arctic blue lettering) edited by | W. H. Auden. On right-hand side arctic blue band down cover with lettering in white: FABER paper covered EDITIONS. Spine lettering: · Selected Poems of Louis MacNeice · (white lettering in arctic blue band) FABER. Back cover, arctic blue band and lettering as front cover, and publisher's list continued from inside back cover.
White wove paper.

22,000 copies printed. Published 10 November 1964, price 6/6.

Contents:
An eclogue for Christmas—Eclogue by a five-barred gate—Elephant trunk—River in spate—Happy families—Spring sunshine—Circe—Spring voices—Snow—Sunday morning—Birmingham—Carrickfergus—The sunlight on the garden—Chess—Eclogue from Iceland—Eclogue between the motherless—Elephants—Bagpipe music—Christmas shopping—The Hebrides—Autumn journal (cantos. II, IV, IX, XXIV)—Stylite—Entirely—London rain—Order to view—Flight of the heart—Autobiography—Evening in Connecticut—Night club—The dowser—Prayer before birth—Troll's courtship—Neutrality—The mixer—Nostalgia—When we were children—Corner seat—Littoral—The cromlech—Under the mountain—Aubade for

infants—The cyclist—Woods—Autolycus—Hands and eyes—Slow movement—Western landscape—Mahabalipuram—The window—*from* Donegal tryptich—The once-in-passing—The here-and-never—Wessex guidebook—Beni Hasan—*from* Jigsaws—The other wing—The burnt bridge—House on a cliff—Figure of eight—*from* Visitations—Invocation—The slow starter—on the Venerable Bede—on the Grettir saga—on the Njal saga—on the four masters—Dandelions—Cats—Corncrakes—The sea—The park—The lake in the park—Dogs in the park—Sunday in the park—Jungle clearance Ceylon—Vistas—Reflections—Hold-up—The wiper—The blasphemies—Selva oscurae—Soap suds—The suicide—Pet shop—Flower shop—The taxis—After the crash—Another cold May—Ravenna—Charon—The introduction—The habits—Greyness is all—*from* Memoranda to Horace—Coda—*from* The Agamemnon of Aeschylus—Solvitur acris hiems

A36a   THE STRINGS ARE FALSE   1965

First edition:
THE STRINGS ARE FALSE | *An Unfinished Autobiography* | by | LOUIS MACNEICE | FABER AND FABER | 24 Russell Square | London

Collation: 22×15 cm. 1–188 144 leaves pp*1*–6 7 8 9 *10* 11–15 *16* 17–288

pp*1*–2 blank p*3* half-title p*4* list of works by LM p*5* title-page p*6* Printed in Great Britain by | Western Printing Services Limited Bristol p*7* Contents p*8* blank p*9* list of illus. p*10* blank pp11–15 Editor's preface p*16* blank pp17–215 The Strings are False pp216–238 Appendix A: Landscapes of Childhood and Youth pp239–284 Appendix B: LM at Marlborough and Oxford by John Hilton pp258–288 Index.
Half-tone illus opp. p4 and p62.

Rose pink cloth binding, gold lettering stamped across spine: (on black label encased in thin gold lines) THE | STRINGS | ARE | FALSE (and then on spine) LOUIS | MACNEICE | FABER. White dustjacket: (crimson) Louis MacNeice | [dark violet band across cover, continued up foredge to top of cover] | *THE* | *STRINGS* | *ARE* | *FALSE* (in grass green). Spine lettering: dark violet band (grass green) Louis | MacNeice | [dark violet band] | (crimson) THE STRINGS | ARE FALSE | [dark violet band] | (grass green across spine) Faber. List of works by LM on back of jacket.
White wove paper.

4,000 copies printed. Published 11 November 1965, price 30/-.

Notes:
1. Strings are False composed at beginning of 2nd World War, Landscapes of Childhood and Youth, a fragment of Countries in the Air, commissioned by Faber in 1957.
2. The Editor is E. R. Dodds.

A36b THE STRINGS ARE FALSE 1966

First American edition:
THE STRINGS ARE FALSE | *An Unfinished Autobiography* | by | LOUIS MACNEICE | 1966 | OXFORD UNIVERSITY PRESS | NEW YORK

Collation: 21.5 × 14.5 cm. 1–9^{16} 144 leaves pp*3–16* 17–288

p*3* half-title p*4* list of works by LM p*5* blank p*6* half-tone illus. of LM p*7* title-page p*8* Printed in the United States of America p*9* Contents list p*10* blank p*11–15* Editor's preface p*16* blank pp17–215 The Strings are False pp216–238 Appendix A pp239–284 Appendix B pp285–288 Index.
[Half-tone illus. of Elizabeth and Louis MacNeice is between pp62 and 63 and forms part of gathering].

Off-white cloth binding, aircraft blue lettering down spine: [two thin brilliant green lines across spine] Louis MacNeice [green lettering] The Strings Are False [then blue lettering across spine] Oxford. Dustjacket is white with green and blue grain finish. Front cover: [blue] Louis | MacNeice | [green] The Strings | Are False. Spine: [green] Louis MacNeice [blue] The Strings Are False [green across spine] Oxford. List of works by LM on back of jacket.
White wove paper.

3,075 copies printed. Published 29 September 1966, price $6.00.

Notes: as first edition

A37 VARIETIES OF PARABLE 1965

First edition:
VARIETIES OF | PARABLE BY | LOUIS MACNEICE | CAMBRIDGE | AT THE UNIVERSITY PRESS | 1965

Collation: 20.5 × 13.5 cm. 11^4 1–10^8 (gatherings 1–10 also signed MVP) 84 leaves pp*i–iv* v *vi* vii *viii* 1–156 *157–160* p*i* half-title p*ii* blank p*iii* title-page p*iv* PUBLISHED BY | THE SYNDICS OF THE CAMBRIDGE UNIVERSITY PRESS (and then lower down) *Printed in Great Britain at the University Printing House, Cambridge | Brooke Crutchley, University Printer* pv Preface p*vi* blank p*vii* Contents p*viii* blank pp1-151 text p152 Bibliography pp153-157 Index pp*158-160* blank.

Black cloth binding, gold lettering stamped up spine: CAMBRIDGE *Varieties of Parable · MacNeice*. Terra cotta dustjacket with eau-de-nil back cover. Front cover, black lettering: LOUIS | MACNEICE | [printer's device: spiral in eau-de-nil] | Varieties | Of | Parable | [printer's device as above] | CAMBRIDGE | UNIVERSITY PRESS. Lettering down spine: (black) MACNEICE (eau-de-nil) *Varieties of Parable* (black) *Cambridge*. Advertisement for CUP book on back of jacket.
White wove paper.

5,000 copies printed. Published 11 November 1965, price 22/6, in U.S.A. $4.50.

Note: First presented as the Clark Lectures at Cambridge University in the spring of 1963.

A38a   COLLECTED POEMS OF LOUIS MACNEICE   1966

First edition:
The Collected Poems of | LOUIS MACNEICE | [short swelled rule] | edited by E. R. Dodds | FABER & FABER | 24 Russell Square London

Collation: 21.5 × 14 cm. 1–36⁸ 37¹⁰ 298 leaves pp*i–iv* v–xviii 1–2 3–575 576–578

p*i* half-title p*ii* list of works by LM p*iii* title-page p*iv* *Printed in Great Britain by* | *Western Printing Services Limited, Bristol* ppv–xiii Contents pxiv LM's preface to CP 1925-1948 ppxv–xvi Editor's preface ppxvii–xviii To Hedli (p) p*1* I | *Juvenilia,* 1925–1929 p*2* blank pp3–559 text pp560–561 Appendix I p562 Appendix II pp563–566 Index of titles pp567–575 Index of first lines pp*576–578* blank.

Light orange cloth binding, gold lettering stamped across spine: The | Collected | Poems | of | Louis | MacNeice | [short swelled rule] | *edited by* | E. R. Dodds | FABER. Cream dustjacket. Front cover, black lettering on light orange rectangle, at each short end signal red thick lines with concave ends: Collected | POEMS | of | Louis |

MacNeice. Spine lettering: [signal red lines with concave ends] | Collected | Poems of | [then on orange band, lettering down spine] Louis MacNeice | [then off band and across spine] Faber & | Faber | [signal red line with concave ends].
List of works by LM on back of jacket.
White wove paper.

5,560 copies printed. Published 14 December 1966, price 63/-.

Contents:
The creditor—Trains in the distance—Genesis—Glass falling—Poussin—Evening indoors—Elephant trunk—River in spate—Candles—Nocturne—The lugubrious, salubrious seaside—Happy families — Breaking webs — Mahavveray — Spring sunshine — Cradle song for Miriam—Mayfly—Belfast—Birmingham—Turfstacks—Upon this beach—Circe—Spring voices—Museums—A contact—Nature morte—To a communist—The individualist speaks—Sunday morning—August—The glacier—Perseus—An April manifesto—Morning sun—Cuckoo—Train to Dublin—Intimations of mortality—Wolves—Aubade—Snow—An eclogue for Christmas—Eclogue by a five-barred gate—Eclogue from Iceland—Eclogue between the motherless—Valediction—Ode—Homage to clichés—Letter to Graham and Anna—The Hebrides—Carrickfergus—Iceland—Passage steamer—Postscript to Iceland—Sand in the air—Now that the shapes of mist—Hidden ice—The oracle—Riding in cars—War heroes—Pindar is dead—Les neiges d'antan—Empty shoes—The jingles of the morning—Finale—Taken for granted—The brandy glass—The sunlight on the garden—June thunder—The heated minutes—Leaving Barra—Trilogy for X—Chess—Circus—Christmas shopping—Bagpipe music—Autumn journal—Prognosis—Stylite—Entirely—Plant and phantom—The British Museum Reading Room—London rain—Dublin—Cushendun—Sligo and Galway—Why, now it has happened—Meeting point—A toast—Order to view—The old story—Les sylphides—The gardener—Christina—Provence—The preacher—Débâcle—Death of an actress—Bar room matins—Flight of the heart—Refugees—Jehu—The deathwish — Autobiography — Conversation — The ear — Evening in Connecticut—Barcelona in wartime—Business men—Night club—Didymus—Plain speaking—Perdita—The dowser—The return—Cradle song for Eleanor—Prayer for birth—Precursors—Explorations — Mutations — Brother fire — The trolls — Troll's courtship—The revenant—Convoy—Whit Monday—Swingsong—Bottleneck—Neutrality—The conscript—The news-reel

—Nuts in May—The mixer—Nostalgia—Babel—Schizophrene—Alcohol—The libertine—Epitaph for liberal poets—The satirist—This way out—Thyestes—Prayer in mid-passage—Prospect—The springboard—When we were children—The streets of Laredo—Hiatus—Corner seat—Aftermath—Twelfth night—Bluebells—Tam cari capitis—The National Gallery—Littoral—The cromlech—Carrick revisited—Slum song—The Strand—Last before America—Under the mountain—No more sea—Godfather—Aubade for infants—The cyclist—Woods—Elegy for minor poets—Autolycus—Street scene—Relics—The drunkard—Hands and eyes—Place of a skull—Slow movement—Carol—Plurality—The casualty—The kingdom—Western landscape—The Stygian banks—Letter from India—The North Sea—Mahabalipuram—The window—Suite for recorders—Areopagus—Cock o' the north—Didymus—Our sister water—The island—Day of renewal—Day of returning—The death of a cat—Flowers in the interval—Autumn sequel—To the public—To posterity—April fool—Dreams in middle age—Sailing orders—Donegal tryptich—The left-behind—The back-again—The gone-tomorrow—The once-in-passing—The here-and-never—Wessex guidebook—The rest house—Beni Hasan—Return to Lahore—Visit to Rouen—Time for a smoke—Jigsaws i–v—Easter returns—The other wing—The burnt bridge—The tree of guilt—House on a cliff—Figure of eight—Death of an old lady—Visitations i–vii—Apple blossom—Invocation—The riddle—Notes for a biography—The slow starter—Il piccolo rifiuto—The messiah—The Atlantic tunnel—Homage to Wren—Rites of war—Jericho—Yours next—On the Venerable Bede—On the Grettir saga—On the Njal saga—On the four masters—Darts—Shove halfpenny—Vingt-et-un — Crossword puzzles — Idle talk — Country weekend — Dandelions—Cats—Corncrakes—The sea—North wind—East wind—West wind—South wind—The park—The lake in the park—Dogs in the park—Sunday in the park—Windowscape—Solstice—Indian village—Jungle clearance Ceylon—Half truth from Capetown—Solitary travel—Old masters abroad—Icebergs—Vistas—Variation on Heraclitus—Reflections—Hold-up—Restaurant car—The wiper—The wall—The snow man—The truisms—The blasphemies—Bad dream—Good dream—Selva oscura—All over again—Soap suds—Déjà vu—Round the corner—The suicide—Perspectives—Château Jackson—Pet shop—Flower shop—In lieu—The taxis—The grey ones—After the crash—Spring cleaning—Another cold May—The pale panther—Rechauffé—Ravenna—Constant—October in Bloomsbury—

New Jerusalem—Charon—The introduction—Birthright—Children's games—Tree party—Sports page—The habits—Greyness is all—As in their time—This is the life—Budgie—Memoranda to Horace—Star gazer—Goodbye to London—Off the peg—Coda—Thalassa
Translations:
Three odes of Horace: *Solvitur acris hiems—Requam memento—Carpe diem*—Four medieval Latin poems: *Jam lucis orto sidine—Corona virginium—Ut quid iubes, pusiole—Meum est propositum*—Three poems in defeat, from the French of Louis Aragon: *The lilacs and the roses—The occupied zone—Richard Coeur-de-Lion*—The legend of the dead soldier, from the German of Bertolt Brecht

A38b COLLECTED POEMS OF LOUIS MACNEICE 1967

First American edition:
The Collected Poems of | LOUIS MACNEICE | [short swelled rule] | edited by E. R. Dodds | New York | OXFORD UNIVERSITY PRESS | 1967

Collation: 21.5 × 14 cm. $1-18^{16}$ 19^{12} 300 leaves pp*i–iv* v–xviii 1–2 3–575 576–582

Contents: As first edition but p*iv Printed in the United States of America;* pp576–582 blank

Off-white cloth binding, lettering down spine: [signal red two thin rules across spine] [golden brown] The Collected Poems of [red] Louis MacNeice [then brown across spine] Oxford. Dust-jacket is white with red and brown grain finish. Front cover: [red] The | Collected | Poems | [brown] of | Louis | MacNeice. Spine, lettering down: [brown] The Collected Poems [red] of Louis MacNeice [brown across spine] Oxford. List of works by LM on back of jacket.
White wove paper.

2,575 copies printed. Published 19 January 1967, price $9.75.
2,600 copies printed in 2nd impression, price $10.75.

A39a ONE FOR THE GRAVE 1968

First edition:
One for the Grave | *a modern morality play* | by | LOUIS MACNEICE | FABER AND FABER | 24 Russell Square | London

Collation: 22×14 cm. A^8 B–E^8 F^6 46 leaves pp*1*–*6* 7–8 *9*–*10* 11 12 13–90 *91*–*92*

pp*1*–*2* blank p*3* half-title p*4* list of works by LM p*5* title-page p*6* *Printed in Great Britain by | Latimer Trend & Co Ltd Plymouth* pp7–8 Prefatory note and original cast p*9* performing right restrictions p*10* blank p*11* Characters p*12* blank pp13–14 Notes by LM pp15–89 text p90 Notes by Hedli MacNeice pp*91*–*92* blank.

'Strong blue' cloth binding, gold lettering stamped down spine: Louis MacNeice · ONE FOR THE GRAVE Faber. Pale cream dust-jacket. black lettering: (on verdigris green background) Louis | MacNeice | (on light orange background) ONE | FOR THE | GRAVE | [swelled rule]. Spine lettering: (verdigris green) Louis MacNeice (black) One for the Grave (then in orange across the spine) Faber. List of works by LM on back of jacket.

4,050 copies printed. Published 29 January 1968, price 21/-.

Notes: Play written 1958–59, unrevised, first performed October 1966. Note from p7:-
The world premiere was given at the Abbey Theatre | during the Dublin Theatre Festival, 1966. The director was | Frank Dermody; the settings were by Liam Miller and the | music by Gerard Victory. First published in *The Massachusetts Review*, Winter 1967.

A39b   ONE FOR THE GRAVE   1968

First American issue:
One for the Grave | *a modern morality play* | by | LOUIS MACNEICE | New York | OXFORD UNIVERSITY PRESS | 1968

Collation: As first edition

Contents: As first edition *but* p*6* *Printed in Great Britain*

Description as first edition *but* in lettering on spine of binding 'Oxford' replaces 'Faber'

1,796 copies imported. Published 14 March 1968, price $4.50.

A40   PERSONS FROM PORLOCK   1969

First edition:
Louis MacNeice | Persons from Porlock | AND OTHER PLAYS FOR RADIO | WITH AN INTRODUCTION | BY W. H. AUDEN | British Broadcasting Corporation

Collation: 25×16 cm. $A*A^{4.12}$ B*B–D*$D^{4.12}$ E^8 72 leaves pp*1–6 7–9 10–12 13*–144

p*1* half-title p*2* blank p*3* title-page p*4* Printed in England by The Broadwater Press Limited p*5* Contents p*6* blank pp7–9 Foreword p*10* blank p*11* Enter Caesar | A study of the evolution and background of | the first great dictator of the modern type p*12* Cast and details of 1st performance pp13–42 text p*43* East of the Sun and West of the Moon | A Norwegian Folk Tale p*44* Cast and details of 1st performance pp45–70 text p*71* They Met on Good Friday | A Sceptical Historical Romance p*72* Cast and details of 1st performance pp73–106 text p*107* Persons from Porlock | The Story of a Painter p*108* Cast and details of 1st performance pp109–144 text.

Forest green cloth binding, gold lettering stamped down spine between thin gold parallel lines: LOUIS MACNEICE PERSONS FROM PORLOCK BBC. White dustjacket, black lettering. Front cover, thin black line as frame to type area: LOUIS | MACNEICE | [thick black line] | [thin black line, then light orange area imperfectly covering the next three words] PERSONS | FROM | PORLOCK | [thin black parallel lines] | and other plays for radio | [thick black line] | [then at foot of cover on dark violet area] Introduction by W. H. Auden. Lettering down spine between thin black parallel lines: (dark violet lettering) LOUIS MACNEICE (black) PERSONS FROM PORLOCK (dark violet lettering) BBC. Details of other BBC publications on back of jacket.
White wove paper.

2,500 copies printed. Published September 1969, price 35/-.

Notes: First performances:

Enter Caesar	Home Service	20 September 1946
East of the Sun and West of the Moon	Third Programme	25 July 1959
They met on Good Friday	,,	8 December 1959
Persons from Porlock	,,	30 August 1963

B

CONTRIBUTIONS TO BOOKS AND PERIODICALS

TERMINAL DATE: DECEMBER 1967

* Items from William MacKinnon's 'Bibliography of Louis MacNeice' *in* 'The bulletin of bibliography' April–June 1970 pp51–2. (Items verified by Sir Anthony Blunt)

† Items verified by John Hilton

1924

B1	October 23	The Marlburian	pp144–5 'The dissolution of Valhalla'
B2	October 23	The Marlburian	'Death of a prominent businessman'*
B3	October 23	The Marlburian	'The story of the "Great Triobel Clan" as created by Mr. Schinabel' (prose)*
B4	November 20	The Marlburian	'Babylon'*
B5	November 20	The Marlburian	'The ways are green and gorgons creep'*

1925

B6	March 11	The Marlburian	'The witch of Widdigofree'*
B7	June 24	The Marlburian	'Circe'*
B8	October 22	The Marlburian	pp117–8 'The devil'
B9	October 22	The Marlburian	'Nocturne'*
B10	November 19	The Marlburian	'Cradle song'*

1926

B11	February 17	The Marlburian	p17 'And the spirit returns'
B12	March 10	The Marlburian	'Windows in the ink' (prose)*
B13	March 29	The Marlburian	'Jam of Aganippe' (prose)*
B14	March 29	The Marlburian	'Jack and the beanstalk'*
B15	March 29	The Marlburian	'Spring'
B16	May 26	The Marlburian	pp65–66 'Gardener melancholy'
B17	May 26	The Marlburian	'Moon-fishery: a dialogue'*
B18	May 26	The Marlburian	'Apollo on the Old Bath Road I'*
B19	May 26	The Marlburian	'Miss Ambergris and King Perhaps'*

B20	June 23	The Marlburian	'Apollo on the Old Bath Road II–V'*
B21	July 26	The Marlburian	p115 'But genius finds the commonplace a silver rhyme' (entered for the Furneaux Prize)
B22	July 26	The Marlburian	'Apollo on the Old Bath Road VI–X'*
B23	October 30	The Cherwell	p81 'Seaside'
B24	November 13	The Cherwell	p145 'Harvest thanksgiving'
B25	December 4	The Cherwell	p251 'Fires of hell' (prose)
B26	December 11	The Cherwell	p303 'In the cathedral: *The voluptary—The church-warden*'

1927

B27 'Υννοι οέντον—Harvest thanksgiving—This tournament' *in* 'Oxford Poetry 1927' ed. by W. H. Auden and C. D. Lewis. Pub. O.U.P. pp18–20

B28	June 11	The Cherwell	p176 'Song in the back of the mind'
B29	June 11	The Cherwell	pp185–6 'The front door of ivorys' (prose)*
B30	October 22	The Cherwell	p24 'Reading by candle-light: Monday, October 17th, 1927'

1928

B31 'Reading by candle-light—Glass falling—Happy families—Impermanent creativeness' *in* 'Oxford Poetry 1928' ed. by Clere Parsons. Pub. O.U.P. pp 30–35

1929

B32 'Spring sunshine—Address from my death-bed to Dr. Bruno, the concrete universal—Cradle song—Laburnum' *in* 'Oxford Poetry 1929' ed. by Louis MacNeice and Stephen Spender.
Pub. O.U.P. pp24–29

B33	February	Sir Galahad	p9 'Epitaph for Louis'; p15 'Garlon and Galahad' (prose); p18 'Paradise Lost' signed John Bogus Rosifer, Keble College†
B34	May	Sir Galahad	pp3–4 'Our god bogus' (prose); p4 'From down here'; p9 'Take away that bathos' signed Anon.†; p22 'Saul'
B35	May 18	Literary Digest	p34 'Impermanent creativeness'

1930

B36 'Utopia—Hinges kill themselves—Threnody' *in* 'Oxford Poetry 1930' ed. by Stephen Spender and Bernard Spencer. Pub. O.U.P. pp20–23

B37	February	Oxford Outlook	pp421–9 'Neurospastoumenos'
B38	May	Oxford Outlook	pp489–90 'The prodigal son, or, The dog returns to his vomit'

1932

B39	June	This Quarter	pp610–3 'Sleep—Belfast—Vitreamque Circen'

1933

B40	January	New Verse	pp2–3 'Turn again Worthington'; pp10–11 'Everyman his own Pygmalion'
B41	March	New Verse	pp14–15 'Poem' ('Turfstacks')
B42	October 5	New Verse	pp6–7 'Poem (The glacier) —August a la Poussin'

B43	November 29	The Listener	p844 'The individualist speaks'
B44	December	New Verse	pp6–7 'Poem' (Nature Mort); pp18–19 rev. 'Life of the dead' by Laura Riding

1934

B45	February	New Verse	pp3–4 'Birmingham'
B46	April	New Verse	pp3–7 'An eclogue for Christmas'
B47	April/ September	Life and Letters	pp352–4 'Valediction: an eclogue'
B48	May	American Review	pp253–9 'An eclogue for Christmas'
B49	May 16	The Listener	p834 'Springpiece'
B50	June	Architectural Review	p227 'Birmingham'
B51	June	New Verse	pp18 & 20 rev. 'Poems of Edwin Muir'
B52	October	New Verse	p7 'Answer to an enquiry' (prose)
B53	October/ July 1935	The Criterion	pp161–2 rev. 'Domain of selfhood' by R. V. Feldman
B54	October 17	The Listener	p642 'Perseus'
B55	October 17	New Republic	p268 'An April manifesto'
B56	December	New Verse	pp12–13 'Two poems' (Wolves—Great expectations)

1935

B57 'Poetry today' *in* 'The arts today' ed. by G. Grigson. Pub. Lane pp25–67

B58	February	New Verse	pp2–3 'Train to Dublin'

B59	March 27	The Listener	p480 'Snow'
B60	April	New Verse	pp26–27 'A comment on the technique of G. M. Hopkins'
B61	Spring	Mosiac	pp18–19 'Poems' (To a communist—A contact—The creditor—Perseus)
B62	May 8	The Listener	Supp. pxiv rev. S. Spender's 'Destructive element'
B63	June	New Verse	p7 'Insidiae'; p9 'Cuckoo'
B64	August/September	New Verse	pp17–18 rev. William Empson 'Poems'
B65	December	New Verse	pp7–9 'Some notes on Mr. Yeats's plays'

1936

B66 'Sir Thomas Malory' *in* 'English novelists: a survey of the novel by twenty contemporary novelists' ed. by Derek Verschoyle. Pub. Chatto and Windus pp19–28

B67	February/March	New Verse	pp2–4 'Homage to cliches'; p16 rev. 'The newest Yeats'
B68	March 11	The Listener	p480 'Hidden ice'
B69	August	Group Theatre Paper No. 2	p3 extract from 'Agamemnon'
B70	October	The Criterion	pp120–2 rev. W. B. Yeats 'Dramatis Personae'
B71	November 12	The Times	p10 Letter about rev. of 'The Agamemnon'
B72	December	Group Theatre Paper No. 6	pp3–5 'Extracts from a dialogue (between LM and Rupert Doone, November 22) on the necessity for an active tradition and experiment; p8 'Finale'

GROUP THEATRE PAPER

No. 1   JUNE 1936   Price 1d

NEW ANNOUNCEMENTS

Productions

First production of the Autumn will be a new adaptation by Louis MacNeice of the "Agamemnon of Aeschylus" produced by Rupert Doone. This is a re-translation from the Greek original, an extract of which will appear in the July issue of Group Theatre Paper.

Film Group

New activity of the Group Theatre under the direction of Basil Wright and Rupert Doone.

Chief aim of FILM GROUP is to build up a creative movement in cinema which shall express the aim of the Group Theatre.

In September, FILM GROUP will open with a special performance of films, at a cinema to be announced later, at which certain notable film personalities will speak. Subsequently there will be four similar performances during the winter 1936/7.

Enquiries for subscription: c/o the Group Theatre.

In addition to the Sunday showing of films, there will be a separate activity for those interested in PRODUCTION of cinema, with PROGRAMME as follows:—

FIRST YEAR.

1. Lecture course, covering the practical and theoretical aspects of the film, by well-known producers, directors cameramen and actors.

2. Practical classes on the elements of film production, under the supervision of Wright.

3. Visits to film studios.

4. Regular shows of films illustrating the development of film technique.

SECOND YEAR.

1. Continuation of practical classes.

2. Continuation of film shows.

3. If funds permit, the actual production of short experimental films.

The first course will start in September 1936.

The next issue will contain an article by Basil Wright, detailing the proposed activities of FILM GROUP, the cost of the various courses, and the privileges of GROUP THEATRE members in it.

Group Theatre Paper No. 1, June 1936

SPONSORED BY THE SUNDAY TIMES

THE GROUP THEATRE
In association with the Institute of Contemporary Arts

presents

HOMAGE TO DYLAN THOMAS

A PROGRAMME OF POETRY
DRAMA AND MUSIC

Devised by
LOUIS MACNEICE, RUPERT DOONE, and VERA LINDSAY

Personal tribute written by
DR EDITH SITWELL
and Requiem Canto by LOUIS MACNEICE

Decor by
CERI RICHARDS

Staged by
JOHN MOODY

THE GLOBE THEATRE
LICENSEE AND MANAGER HAROLD GOSLING
Shaftesbury Avenue W1

SUNDAY 24 JANUARY 1954 AT 8 PM

Souvenir programme for 'Homage to Dylan Thomas',
presented by The Group Theatre in 1954
(*see* 'Gramophone Recordings')

B73	Xmas	New Verse	pp8–9 'Iceland'; pp10–13 'Lyrics from a play' (Out of the picture)
B74	December 9	The Listener	p1086 'Poem' (Now that the shapes of mist.)

1937

B75 'Subject in modern poetry' *in* English Associations Essays Volume 22 pp144–158

B76	January	Group Theatre Paper No. 7	pp2–3 'A parable' (this forms the conclusion of the dialogue between LM and Rupert Doone)
B77	January 27	The Listener	p151 'Song' (Sunlight on the garden)
B78	February/April	London Mercury	pp430–1 rev. J. Cocteau 'Infernal machine'
B79	March	London Mercury	pp451–3 'An epilogue'
B80	March 31	The Listener	p603 'Passage steamer'
B81	June 25	The Spectator	p1187 'Bradford Greek play: Oedipus Tyrannus'
B82	June 30	The Listener	p1306 'Sonnet'
B83	July	The Criterion	pp698 rev. 'The notebooks and papers of Gerard Manley Hopkins'
B84	September 15	The Listener	p573 'The heated minutes'
B85	Autumn	New Writing 4	p6 'June thunder'
B86	October 6	The Listener	pp718–720 'The Hebrides: a tripper's commentary'
B87	October 13	The Listener	Supp. pviii rev. A. Waley 'Book of songs'
B88	November	New Verse	pp11–13 'Letter to W. H. Auden'
B89	November 17	The Listener	p1089 'Solvitur acris hiems'

B90	December 29	The Listener	pp1407–8 'In defence of vulgarity'

1938

B91 'The play and the audience' *in* 'Footnotes to the theatre' ed. by R. D. Charques. Pub. Peter Davies pp32–43.

B92	January	New Verse	pp2–3 'Bagpipe music'; pp12–13 'Perchists'; p18 'Letter to editor' (complaint about rev. of Group Theatre)
B93	July 9	T.L.S.	Supp. pi 'Departure platform'
B94	Autumn	New Verse	p7 'A statement' (about political commitment)
B95	Autumn	New Writing N.S.I.	pp98–101 'Three poems' ('When clerks and navvies fondle'—'And love hangs still'—'March gave clear days')
B96	December 8	The Listener	Supp. pviii rev. (Poetry of Graves, Crane and S. Smith)

1939

B97 'Remembering Spain' *in* 'Poems for Spain' ed. by Stephen Spender and John Lehmann. Pub. Hogarth pp97–100

B98	January 20	The Spectator	p84 'Today in Barcelona' (prose)
B99	February	Poetry London	p12 'Autumn Journal: Canto II'
B100	March 10	The Spectator	p404 theatre rev. 'Antigone of Sophocles'
B101	April	Poetry London	pp8–9 'First chorus from the Hippolytus of Euripidies'
B102	Spring	Partisan Review	pp60–1 'Autumn Journal: Canto II'

B103	May	New Verse	pp58–60 'Painters and poets' (letter about William Coldstream)
B104	May 3	New Republic	pp384–5 'Original sin' (rev. of T. S. Eliot 'The Reunion')
B105	July 27	N.S.N.	pp185–6 'Tendencies in modern poetry: a discussion between Prof. Higgins and LM'
B106	August 12	N.S.N.	p245 'Les sylphides'
B107	August 25	The Spectator	p285 'Primrose Hill'
B108	October 21	N.S.N.	p559 'Galway'
B109	November 18	N.S.N.	p704 'September evening'
B110	December 7	The Listener	Supp. pxv rev. John Hadfield 'Christmas Companion'
B111	December 9	N.S.N.	p820 'Shopping—Idealist'
B112	Christmas	New Writing N.S.3	pp78–82 'Four poems' (Prognosis—Novelette—Meeting Point—A toast)

1940

B113   'Take me for your occassion and mute machine—The knowledge without process—Bring me out of the cave' *in* 'The Lyric psalter: the modern reader's Book of Psalms'. Pub. N.Y., Liveright pp63, 282, 285.

B114	January	Horizon	pp13–14 'Cushendun—The British Museum Reading-Room'
B115	January 6	N.S.N.	p11 'Clock—Interregnum'
B116	February	Horizon	pp122–3 'Dublin'
B117	March	Living Age	p16 'Interregnum'
B118	March 25	New Republic	p412 'The poet in England today'

B119	April	National Review	p451 'Poem in seven spaces'
B120	April 29	New Republic	p583 'Christina'
B121	Spring	Furioso	p12 'London rain'; p14 'Conversation'
B122	May	Poetry (Chicago)	pp59–68 'Prognosis—Obituary—O'Connell Bridge—Entirely—Order to view—I am that I am—Three thousand miles—The British Museum Reading-Room—Perdita—Stylite'
B123	May/June	Poetry London	p169 'Troll's courtship'
B124	May 20	New Republic	p678 'Radio'
B125	May 27	New Republic	p719 'Return'
B126	June 3	New Republic	p767 'Leaves from a journal—November afternoon—Clock'
B127	June 24	New Republic	pp862–3 rev. 'Yeat's Epitaph'
B128	July	Horizon	p462 'American letter' (prose)
B129	July/August	Partisan Review	pp315–6 'The preacher'
B130	September 14	The Nation	p220 'The Ear'
B131	September 16	New Republic	p390 'The death-wish'
B132	October	Living Age	p181 'The British Museum Reading-Room'
B133	October 21	New Republic	p562 'Night club'
B134	November 2	The Nation	p422 'Novelette'
B135	November 11	New Republic	p651 'Flight of the heart'
B136	November 30	New Yorker	p32 'Ballade of England'
B137	November/December	Partisan Review	pp430–9 'Oxford in the twenties'

B138	December	Harpers Bazaar	p121 'Death of an actress'
B139	December 28	N.S.N.	p78 'Death of an actress'

1941

B140	'John Keats' *in* 'Fifteen poets' Pub. O.U.P. pp351–354		
B141	January	Horizon	pp10–12 'Plurality'
B142	January	Penguin New Writing 2	p63 'June thunder'
B142	January 4	New Yorker	p24 'Barroom matins'
B143	January 11	N.S.N.	p34 'Conversation'
B144	January 18	N.S.N.	p66 rev. 'Golden treasury of Scottish poetry'
B145	January 20	New Republic	p81 'Provence'
B146	January 25	New Yorker	p21 'The sense of smell'
B147	January 31	The Spectator	p116 'The cinema' ('Freedom radio')
B148	February	Horizon	pp110–117 'Traveller's return'
B149	February 7	The Spectator	p152 rev. 'Through stained glass' (Masefield on Yeats)
B150	February 14	The Spectator	p172 'The cinema' ('Tin Pan Alley'—'Arise my love'—'Arizona')
B151	February 22	N.S.N.	p184 'The Return'
B152	March	Horizon	pp207–210 'Touching America' (prose)
B153	March	Penguin New Writing 4	pp136–7 'March gave clear days'
B154	March 21	The Spectator	p307 'The cinema' ('Angels over Broadway'—'The trail of the vigilantes')
B155	April	Penguin New Writing 5	pp9–15 'The way we live now' (prose)

B156	May	Harpers Bazaar	p134 'Débâcle'
B157	May	Penguin New Writing 6	pp35–36 'Prognosis'
B158	May 3	N.S.N.	pp466–7 rev. 'U.S.A.' ('Who are the Americans' by William D. Whitney)
B159	May 17	N.S.N.	pp512–3 rev 'Autobiographies'
B160	July	Penguin New Writing 8	p67 'Poem' ('And love hung still . . .')
B161	July 5	N.S.N.	p9 'Trolls'
B162	September 1	Harpers Bazaar	p120 'Autobiography—Evening in Connecticut'
B163	November	Penguin New Writing 11	pp38–40 'Meeting point'
B164	Winter	Kenyon Review	pp31–3 'Two poems' (Picture galleries—The Dowser)

1942

B164	September 19	New Yorker	p34 'Straight words to a crooked poet'
B165	October	Poetry (Chicago)	p375 'The Springboard'

1943

B166	January	Horizon	pp7–9 'Epitaph for liberal poets—Alcohol—Babel'
B167	January/February	Poetry London	pp23–4 'Bottleneck—Convoys'
B168	March	Horizon	p148 'The twins'
B169	March	Penguin New Writing 16	pp40–42 'Five war poems' ('Brother-fire—Whitmonday—Neutrality—Nostalgia—The Springboard')

B170 June 12	New Yorker	p20 'Whitmonday'	
B171 Summer	New Writing & Daylight	pp22-3 'Translation of two poems by Louis Aragon (The lilacs and the roses——The unoccupied zone)	
B172 July	Horizon	pp4-5 'Thyestes—Nuts in May'	
B173 October 2	Souvenier: second poetry reading in aid of the Merchant Navy Distress Funds, arranged by Lady Gerald Wellesley ... King Charles Hall, Tunbridge Wells. Programme pp6-8 (Cushendun—County Sligo—Galway—Cushendun again—Babel)		

1944

B178 January	Horizon	p6 'The Libertine'	
B179 January	Penguin New Writing 19	pp73-5 'Two poems' (Schizophrene—Prayer before birth)	
B180 March	Horizon	p150 'Mutations'	
B181 June	Horizon	pp366-7 'The satirist—The mixer'	

1945

B182 May 5	N.S.N.	p293 rev. 'The elusive classics' (Virgil)	
B183 October	Sewanee Review	pp611-29 'Aragon: a little anthology' (The lilacs and the roses—The unoccupied zone—Richard Coeur-de-Lion)	
B184 November	Horizon	pp295-300 'Western landscape—The cromlech—Last before America'	
B185 December	France Libre	pp103-9 'L'ecrivain brittanique et la guerre'	

1946

B186 'Introduction' to 'The golden ass of Apuleius' trans. by William Adlington in the year 1566. Pub. J. Lehmann. ppv–ix

B187 ?	Lagan Vol. 2 No. 1	p19 'Godfather'
B188 ?	New Writing & Daylight 7	pp13–14 'Autolycus'
B189 February	Bell	p940 'Enfant terrible'
B190 April	Penguin New Writing 27	pp38–41 'Three poems' (The streets of Laredo—Slum song—Carrick revisited)
B191 May 10	The Spectator	p484 rev. 'The Knox New Testament
B192 May 18	N.S.N.	p362 rev. 'Pindar'
B193 June 22	Nation	p756 'Aftermath'
B194 September 21	Nation	p324 'Slow movement'
B195 Autumn	Orion Vol. 3 ed. C. D. Lewis, D. Kilham Roberts, Rosamund Lehmann. Pub. Nicholas & Watson pp81–2 'Two poems' (Slow movement—Aftermath)	
B196 December	La cultura nel mondo, Roma.	pp220–4 'The traditional aspect of modern English poetry'

1947

B197 September 28	New York Times Book Review	p1 'The English literary scene today'
B198 Autumn	Penguin New Writing 29	pp19–21 'Two poems' (Bluebells—Elegy for minor poets)
B199 ?	Penguin New Writing 30	pp21–2 'Street scene'
B200 ?	Penguin New Writing 32	p76 'Relics'

1948

B201 'Eliot and the adolescent' *in* 'T. S. Eliot, a symposium, compiled by Richard Marsh and Tambimuttu. Pub. Editions Poetry pp146-151

B202	?	Penguin New Writing 33	pp87-8 'Autolycus'
B203	?	Penguin New Writing 34	pp16-9 'Letter from India'
B204	?	Windmill No. 9	pp38-42 'An alphabet of literary prejudices'
B205	March 13	N.S.N.	p218 rev. 'Indian art'
B206	June	Horizon	p383 'The National Gallery'
B207	June/July	Poetry London	p4 'Twelfth night—Place of a skull'
B208	September 2	The Listener	pp346-7 'English poetry today'
B209	September 11	N.S.N.	p213 'The North Sea'
B210	December 4	N.S.N.	p481 'Mahabalipuram'

1949

B211 'Experiences with images' *in* 'Orpheus Vol. 2' ed. by John Lehmann. Pub. by J. Lehmann pp124-132.

B212	?	Botteghe Oscure, No. 4	pp378-85 'The crash landing'
B213	February 19	N.S.N.	pp184-5 rev. 'An Irish proletarian' (Sean O'Casey)
B214	April 2	N.S.N.	p334 rev. 'An Indian ride' (M. Lyall)
B215	May	Poetry London	pp23-5 rev. 'Selected poems of John Betjemann'
B216	June 11	N.S.N.	p618 rev. 'A guide book for the educated (Rose MacAuley)
B217	August	Partisan Review	pp837-41 'Window'

B218	October 8	N.S.N.	pp380–1 'Poetry, the public and the critic'

1951

B219	June 23	N.S.N.	p712 'Day of returning'

1952

B220	March 15	N.S.N.	p308 'The death of a cat'
B221	April 5	N.S.N.	p408 'The real mixer' (Autobiography of Augustus John)
B222	May 17	N.S.N.	pp591–2 rev. 'About Ireland'
B223	June 7	N.S.N.	p681 rev. 'Sharks Ltd'. (Gavin Maxwell)
B224	August 30	N.S.N.	p242 rev. 'The bardic strain' (Bowra's Heroic Poetry)
B225	September 13	N.S.N.	pp293–4 rev. 'Books in general' (George Herbert)
B226	September 21	The Observer	p8 rev. 'Poets of the English Language'
B227	November 21	T.L.S.	p761 letter 'Literature and the lively arts'
B228	December 19	T.L.S.	p837 letter 'Literature and the lively arts'

1953

B229	April 4	N.S.N.	p402 'The sideliner' (Edward Lear)
B230	May 31	The Observer	p9 'Canzonetta' (poem for the coronation)
B231	August 9	New York Times Book Review	p7 'Poetry needs to be subtle and tough'

Contributions to Books and Periodicals 75

B232	November 7	N.S.N.	p570 rev. 'The other island' (Ireland)
B233	December 5	N.S.N.	p721 rev. 'He weeps by the side of the ocean' (Edward Lear)

1954

B234	January	Encounter	pp12–13 'Dylan Thomas: memoirs and appreciations'
B235	February	London Magazine	pp17–21 'Canto in memoriam Dylan Thomas'; p104 'A note on the mythopoeic use of his friends in "Autumn Sequel"'
B236	April	London Magazine	pp74–7 rev. 'Under Milk Wood'
B237	May 15	N.S.N.	p636 rev. 'Greece and the West'
B238	June 19	N.S.N.	p804 rev. 'In the grand manner' ('The English epic' by Tillyard)
B239	July	Encounter	pp12–14 'Love of women' (*from* Autumn Sequel)
B240	August	London Magazine	pp74–7 rev. (George Herbert)
B241	October 2	N.S.N.	p398 rev. 'Endless old things' ('Letters of W. B. Yeats')
B242	December	Encounter	pp14–16 'Handful of snapshots'

1955

B243	February	London Magazine	pp17–19 'Donegal triptych'
B244	May	London Magazine	pp106–9 rev. (Dylan Thomas)
B245	May 16	New Republic	pp26–7 'Canto XVIII' (Autumn Sequel)

B246 September	London Magazine	p69 (letter concerning rev. of 'Autumn Sequel'); pp71–4 rev. (R. Jarrell and C. M. Bowra)
B247 November	London Magazine	pp17–20 'Visitations'

1956

B248 'Visitations' *in* 'New Poems 1956' ed. by Stephen Spender *et al* Pub. Hutchinson pp36–42.

B249 April	London Magazine	pp12–14 'Four poems of place' (The resthouse—Beni Hassan—Return to Lahore—Wessex guidebook)
B250 April 21	N.S.N.	pp423–4 rev. 'What vomit had John Keats' (Dylan Thomas)
B251 August	London Magazine	pp59–62 rev. (The Russet coat—John Clare)
B252 September	London Magazine	pp23–4 'Two Poems' (Easter returns—Death of an old lady)

1957

B253 March 16	N.S.N.	pp346–7 rev. 'Indian approaches'
B254 April	London Magazine	pp52–5 'Lost generations?'
B255 May	Poetry Book Society Bulletin 14	p*1* 'Visitations' (note on volume)
B256 June 8	N.S.N.	p741 rev. 'Fragments I have shored' (Caitlin Thomas)
B257 November	London Magazine	pp73–5 rev. (Two books on James Joyce)

1958

B258 'New Poems 1958' edited by Bonamy Dobree, Louis MacNeice and Phillip Larkin'. Pub. Michael Joseph.

B259	May	London Magazine	p33 'Indian village'
B260	December	London Magazine	pp69–75 rev. 'Variorum edition of W. B. Yeats'

1959

B261	February 28	N.S.N.	pp286 & 288 'Talking about Rugby'
B262	April	London Magazine	pp36–9 'Notes for a biography'
B263	November	London Magazine	pp37–40 'Country Weekend'
B264	December	Encounter	p34 'Half-truth from Cape Town'

1960

B265 'Dylan Thomas' *in* 'Casebook on Dylan Thomas' ed. Malcolm Brinnin. Pub. N.Y., Cromwell pp282–4

B266 'Dylan Thomas' *in* 'Dylan Thomas: the legend and the poet' ed. E. W. Tedlock. Pub. Heinemann pp85–7

B267	January 16	N.S.N.	p80 rev. 'Twin to drink?' (rugby)
B268	February 12	The Spectator	pp225–6 rev. 'Poetry of this age' (J. M. Cohen)
B269	May	London Magazine	pp12–14 'Poems' (Reflections—Restaurant car—The wiper)
B270	May 22	The Observer	p20 'Apple blossom'
B271	June	Encounter	p30 'Solitary travel'
B272	June 4	N.S.N.	p828 'Bad dream'
B273	June 26	The Observer	p27 'The truisms'
B274	August	London Magazine	p70 rev. (Yeats and Synge)
B275	August 28	The Observer	p27 'Selva oscure'
B276	October 15	N.S.N.	p574 'Jericho'
B277	October 22	N.S.N.	pp623–4 rev. 'Out of ugliness' (W. Owen)

B278 December 17   N.S.N.   pp978–9 rev. 'A modern
                                        odyssey' (G. Seferis)

1961

B279 'When I was twenty-one' *in* 'The Saturday Book 21' ed. John
      Hadfield Pub. Hutchinson pp230–9

B280 February   Poetry Book   'Solstices' (note on volume)
                    Society Bulletin 28

B281 February 10   N.S.N.   p210 'That chair of poetry'
B282 March   London Magazine   p12 'Sleeping winds'
B283 March 5   The Observer   p30 'The slow starter'
B284 June 30   N.S.N.   p1054 'In lieu—Flower
                                        shop'
B285 July 7   N.S.N.   pp27–8 T.V. rev. 'Godot
                                        on T.V.'
B286 July 14   T.L.S.   Supp. pii 'Perspectives'
B287 July 21   N.S.N.   p95 T.V. rev. 'Look at the
                                        faces'
B288 August 4   N.S.N.   p164 T.V. rev. 'I got those
                                        cathode blues'
B289 August 17   The Times   p11 'Woods to get lost in'
B290 August 18   N.S.N.   p225 T.V. rev. 'Roll on
                                        reality'
B291 September 1   N.S.N.   p284 T.V. rev. 'Snow and
                                        rock'
B292 September 15 N.S.N.   p358 T.V. rev. 'Two plays
                                        and Spike'
B293 September 29 N.S.N.   pp450–1 T.V. rev. 'Pins
                                        and needles'
B294 October 8   The Observer   p30 'After the crash—The
                                        taxis'
B295 October 26   The Listener   p678 'Two Poems' (The
                                        suicide—Soap suds)
B296 October 27   N.S.N.   p617 'Chateau Jackson'

Contributions to Books and Periodicals

B297	November 24	N.S.N.	p795 rev. 'Come in, Dominic' (Dominic Behan)

1962

B298	February 4	The Observer	p30 'Constant'
B299	February 16	N.S.N.	p239 'Nine new caps'
B300	June 22	N.S.N.	pp911–2 rev. 'C'est la terre'
B301	June 29	N.S.N.	p948 'Under the sugar loaf'
B302	October 4	The Listener	p527 rev. (Fitzgerald's 'Odyssey' and Logue's 'Patrocleia')
B303	November 18	The Observer	p27 'Charon'
B304	December 16	The Observer	p21 'The habits'
B305	December 28	N.S.N.	p934 'Sports page—October in Bloomsbury—New Jerusalem—Budgie'

1963

B306	January 20	The Observer	p23 'Déjà vu'
B307	January 31	The Listener	p213 rev. (G. Hough's 'Preface to Faery Queen)
B308	March 15	N.S.N.	p388 'This is the life'
B309	March 21	The Listener	p531 rev. (J. Stallworthy's 'Between the lines')
B310	May 3	N.S.N.	p679 rev. 'The ould opinioner' (S. O'Casey)
B311	June 7	N.S.N.	p876 'Gael force at Wembley'
B312	June 27	The Listener	p1083 rev. (G. Johnston's 'Saga of Grisli')
B313	July 5	N.S.N.	pp10 & 12 'Great summer sale'
B314	July 12	N.S.N.	p46 rev. 'Frost' (Robert Frost)

B315	August	London Magazine	pp5–7 'Three poems' (Spring cleaning—Star gazer—Goodbye to London)

[Posthumous publications]

B316	September	Poetry Book Society Bulletin	'The Burning Perch' (note on volume)
B317	September 6	N.S.N.	p294 'Memoranda to Horace' (excerpt)
B318	December 12	The Listener	p990 'Childhood memories'

1964

B319	February	London Magazine	p5 'Two Poems' (Thalassa—Carpe Diem)

1967

B320	Winter	Massachusetts Review	pp13–92 'One for the dead' (The first publication of the play 'One for the grave')

Section B
Addenda (December 1972)

1926

December 11	The Cherwell	p329 rev. 'Collected Poems of James Stephens *and* "Transition" by Edwin Muir'

1927

January 29	The Cherwell	p28 rev. 'Autobiographies of Yeats'
February 19	The Cherwell	p129 rev. 'Christopher Marlowe by V. F. Ellis-Fermor'

	March 5	The Cherwell	p168 rev. 'MacDiarmid's "Drunk man looks at a a thistle"'
	May 21	The Cherwell	p88 rev. 'Duncan Dewar's accounts: a student of St. Andrews 100 years ago'
	June 25	The Cherwell	p230 'American universities'

1928

	November	Oxford Outlook	pp171–3 rev. "E. E. Cummings 'Enormous room"; pp184–5 rev. "The Venture"'

1929

	February	Oxford Outlook	pp219–20 'Cradle song'

C
ITEMS ABOUT LOUIS MACNEICE
TERMINAL DATE: DECEMBER 1971

1928

C1 November 21 The Isis pp13–14 D. Batchelor rev. 'Oxford Poetry 1928'

1929

C2 March 28 T.L.S. p263 rev. 'Blind Fireworks'

C3 December 4 The Isis p16 D. Batchelor rev. 'Oxford Poetry 1929'

1930

C4 January 2 T.L.S. p15 rev. 'Oxford Poetry 1929'

1932

C5 November 10 T.L.S. p840 rev. 'Roundabout Way'

C6 December Life and Letters pp480–1 Brian Roberts rev. 'Roundabout Way'

1935

C7 October/November New Verse pp17–19 Stephen Spender rev. 'Poems'

C8 December Scrutiny pp300–2 Frank Chapman rev. 'Poems'

C9 December Life and Letters p17 Edith Sitwell 'Correspondence on the younger English poets'

C10 Winter Poetry Review pp485–7 Arthur Hood 'Mr. L. M. and others'

1936

C11 May Poetry (Chicago) pp115–7 D. Schwartz rev. 'Adroitly naive'

C12 September Group Theatre Paper 3 pp2–3 A[ngela] W[orthy] 'Note on "The Agamemnon"'

C13	October	Group Theatre Paper 4	pp2–3 Rupert Doone 'The production of "The Agamemnon"'
C14	November	Group Theatre Paper 5	p2 P. Burra 'The Agamemnon'
C15	November 2	The Times	p12 rev. production 'The Agamemnon'

1937

C16	March	Scrutiny	pp453–5 H. A. Mason rev. 'The Agamemnon'
C17	May 19	New Republic	p52 Edmund Wilson rev. 'An Agamemnon for an age of dictators'
C18	July 24	T.L.S.	p540 rev. 'Out of the picture'
C19	August 7	T.L.S.	p572 rev. 'Letters from Iceland'
C20	September	Scrutiny	p227 H. L. Bradbrook rev. 'Out of the picture'
C21	November	Poetry (Chicago)	pp104–7 Samuel French Morse rev. 'An end to the abstract' (Out of the picture)
C22	December 6	The Times	p18 rev. production of 'Out of the picture'

1938

C23	January	London Mercury	p331 rev. 'Out of the picture'
C24	January	New Verse	p19 K. A. [llott] rev. 'Out of the picture'
C25	February	Partisan Review	pp56–60 F. O. Matthiewson rev. 'Poems 1937'
C26	March	Poetry (Chicago)	pp339–44 T. C. Wilson rev. 'One of the best' (Poems 1937)

C27	April	Poetry (Chicago)	pp39–42 T. C. Wilson rev. 'Plenty of news' (Letters from Iceland)
C28	April 5	The Times	p10 rev. 'I crossed the Minch'
C29	April 9	T.L.S.	p247 rev. 'I crossed the Minch'
C30	April 23	N.S.N.	pp696 & 698 Desmond Shawe-Taylor rev. 'Alone in the Hebrides' (I crossed the Minch)
C31	May	London Mercury	pp85–6 Janet Adam Smith 'Hetty as a poet' (I crossed the Minch)
C32	May 7	T.L.S.	p314 rev. 'The earth compels'
C33	June	Scrutiny	pp93–5 Geoffrey Walton rev. (I crossed the Minch—The earth compels)
C34	Summer	New Verse	pp17–19 Geoffrey Grigson rev. (I crossed the Minch—The earth compels)
C35	November 12	T.L.S.	p722 rev. 'Zoo'
C36	November 18	The Spectator	p858 Rose Macaulay rev. 'Our captives' (Zoo)
C37	November 19	N.S.N.	pp835–6 G. W. Stonier rev. 'Cigarette cards of London' (Zoo)
C38	December 10	T.L.S.	p282 rev. 'Modern Poetry'; p285 leader 'Modern Poetry'

1939

C39	January	New Verse	pp20–21 Kenneth Allott rev. 'Civilised common-sense (Modern Poetry and Zoo)

C40	January 6	The Guardian	p5 B. I. Evans rev. 'Modern Poetry'
C41	February	Poetry (Chicago)	pp280–3 Samuel French Morse rev. 'Earth compels'
C42	February 4	Notes and Queries	p90 rev. 'Modern Poetry'
C43	February 25	Saturday Review of Literature	p20 Dudley Fitts 'Belles Lettres'
C44	March	Scrutiny	pp437–40 Geoffrey Walton rev. 'Modern Poetry'
C45	March 3	Commonweal	p528 Sister M. Madeleva rev. 'Modern Poetry'
C46	March 18	Christian Science Monitor	p10 rev. 'Modern Poetry'
C47	March 19	New York Times Book Review	p2 Peter Monro Jack 'L.M. on modern poetry'
C48	April 1	N.S.N.	p508 John Lehmann 'A poet on his circle'
C49	April 23	Books	p10 Babette Deutsch rev. 'Modern Poetry'
C50	May	Forum	p271 Mary Colum 'Poetry diminished' (Modern Poetry)
C51	May 20	T.L.S.	p294 rev. 'Autumn Journal'
C52	June	Scrutiny	p72–3 Q. D. Leavis rev. 'Modern Poetry'
C53	June	Scrutiny	p125–8 W. H. Mellers rev. 'Autumnal Journey' (sic)
C54	June 2	The Guardian	p5 Charles Powell rev. 'Autumn Journal'
C55	June 3	N.S.N.	'p782 G. W. Stonier rev. 'Autumn Journal'
C56	June 30	The Spectator	p1140 Desmond Hawkins rev. 'Autumn Journal'

C57	August 16	New Republic	pp52–3 Allen Tate rev. 'Poetry of the will'
C58	Autumn	Kenyon Review	pp468–71 Randell Jarrell 'From that Island'
C59	December	Yale Review	pp398–402 Maynard Mack rev. 'Critical synthesis'
C60	December 3	The Spectator	p1097 Geoffrey Grigson rev. 'Modern Poetry'

1940

C61 Elizabeth Drew and John L. Sweeney 'Direction in Modern Poetry' Pub. N.Y., W. W. Norton pp87–8, 247–9

C62 J. G. Southworth 'Sowing the Spring' Pub. Blackwell pp165–178

C63	January 27	New Yorker	p62 Louise Bogan rev. 'Autumn Journal'
C64	February 10	Saturday Review of Literature	p18 Seldon Rodman rev. 'Autumn Journal'
C65	February 18	New York Times Book Review	p2 P. M. Jack rev. 'Autumn Journal'
C66	Spring	Furioso	pp36–41 A. Wanning 'MacNeice and Auden on the days and nights of our years'
C67	May	Poetry (Chicago)	pp86–94 Julian Symons 'L.M.: the artist as everyman'
C68	May 11	The Nation	pp602–4 John Peale Bishop 'The Hamlet of L.M.'
C69	June 8	T.L.S.	p282 rev. 'The Last Ditch'
C70	June 22	Christian Science Monitor	p12 J. Ritchey 'English poet views the war'
C71	Autumn	Folios New Writing 2	pp11–13 Virginia Woolf 'The leaning tower'

C72	October/ December	Sewanee Review	pp547–552 Stuart G. Brown rev. 'Poetry and tradition' [Modern Poetry]
C73	November	Poetry (Chicago)	pp152–7 David Daiches 'The honest man alone'
C74	November	Poetry London	pp86–7 Stephen Spender rev. 'Autumn Journal'
C75	Winter	Yale Review	p398 Maynard Mack rev. 'Modern Poetry'

1941

C76	February 28	The Spectator	p234 Michael Roberts rev. 'Mr. MacNeice on Yeats'
C77	March	Scrutiny	pp381–3 W. H. Mellers rev. 'Poetry of W. B. Yeats'
C78	March 1	New Yorker	p56 Louise Bogan rev. 'Collected Poems 1925–1940'
C79	March 29	T.L.S.	p150 rev. 'Poetry of Yeats'
C80	April	Life and Letters Today	pp83–6 Maurice Craig rev. 'Poetry of Yeats'
C81	April 13	Books	p19 Babette Deutsch rev. 'Collected Poems 1925–1940'
C82	April 19	T.L.S.	p194 rev. 'Plant and phantom'
C83	April 26	N.S.N.	p440 K. Muir rev. 'Poetry of Yeats'
C84	May/June	Poetry London	pp199–203 Francis Scarfe rev. 'Plant and phantom'
C85	May 3	Saturday Review of Literature	p6 Dudley Fitts rev. 'MacNeice on Yeats'
C86	May 16	Commonweal	pp88–9 James Burnham rev. 'Yeats'

C87	June	Scrutiny	pp91–3 R. G. Lienhardt rev. 'Plant and phantom'
C88	June 1	Books	p10 Babette Deutsch rev. 'Poetry of Yeats'
C89	June 16	New Republic	pp830–2 Conrad Aiken rev. 'Collected Poems 1925–40'
C90	July	Horizon	pp66–71 Kathleen J. Raine rev. 'Poetry of Yeats'

1942

C91   'L.M.: poetry and commonsense' *in* 'Auden and after' by Francis Scarfe Pub. Routledge pp53-67

1943

C92	January	Sewanee Review	pp62–72 S. G. Brown 'Some poems of L.M.'
C93	February 2	The Times	p2 rev. 'Salute to the Red Army'
C94	Summer	New Writing and Daylight 3	pp111–123 Henry Reed 'The end of an impulse'
C95	August 3	The Times	p2 rev. 'Meet the U.S. Army'

1944

C96	January	Poetry (Chicago)	pp218–222 R. Crowder 'Mr. M. and Miss Sitwell'
C97	April 8	T.L.S.	p178 rev. 'Christopher Columbus'
C98	June	Poetry (Chicago)	pp148–158 D. S. Savage 'Poet's perspective'

1945

C99	October 13	The Nation	p380 F. W. Dupee 'Lewis and MacNeice'

1946

C100	February	English Studies	pp29-31 Norman A. Jeffares rev. 'Poetry of Yeats'
C101	April	Poetry (Chicago)	pp44-49 Coleman Rosenberger rev. 'Two conspiracies: M and Aragon' (Springboard)

1947

C102	February 3	T.L.S.	p57 rev. 'Springboard'
C103	June	Bell	pp67-79 Valentine Iremonger 'L.M.: a first study'
C104	Autumn	Poetry Review	pp161-70 R. L. Cook 'L.M.: an appreciation'

1948

C105 'Genesis, or, the poet as maker' *in* 'Poets at work' by Donald A. Stauffer. Pub. N.Y., Harcourt, Brace and Co. pp70-2

C106	June 5	T.L.S.	p315 rev. 'Holes in the sky'

1949

C107	January 29	Saturday Review of Literature	p27 W. V. D. O'Connor 'Master of his idiom'
C108	February	Life and Letters	p111-3 D. Botterill rev. 'Holes in the sky'
C109	August	Poetry (Chicago)	pp301-4 Horace Gregory rev. 'The new January' (Holes in the sky)
C110	September	Poetry London	pp27-8 Terence Tiller rev. 'Holes in the sky'
C111	October 28	T.L.S.	p690 'A poet of our time'
C112	November 18	T.L.S.	p751 J. Yeoman letter in defence of M.

1950

C113	January	Poetry London	pp26–32 H. G. Porteous rev. 'CP'
C114	Autumn	Poetry Review	pp148–9 P. D. Cummins rev. 'CP'

1952

C115 'Wars and rumours' *in* 'Poetry of our time' by Babette Deutsch. Pub. Columbia Univ. Press pp389–42

C116 'L.M.' and 'Yeats the crooked road' *in* 'Responsibilities of the critic' by F. O. Matthiesoen. Pub. O.U.P. pp25–40, 106–111.

C117 N. C. Stageberg and Wallace Anderson 'Poetry as experience' Pub. American Book Co. pp216–221.

C118 'The Oxford boys becalmed' *in* 'The shores of light' by Edmund Wilson Pub. W. H. Allen pp669–73

C119	July 23	The Times	p8 rev. 'Ten burnt offerings'
C120	August 8	T.L.S.	p51 rev. 'Ten burnt offerings'
C121	November/ December	Partisan Review	pp718–22 Fairlie Barker 'Faust, a modern version'

1953

C122	March	Poetry (Chicago)	pp393–7 John McCormick rev. 'Faith and felicity' [Faust]
C123	Spring	Furioso	pp61–4 E. B. Pettet rev. 'Goethe's Faust'
C124	August 21	Commonweal	p495 D. Burham 'Mind of a man'
C125	October	Essays in criticism	pp425–433 R. C. Cragg 'Snow, a philosophical poem'

1954

C126 Edith T. Aney 'British poetry of social protest in the 1930's, the problem of belief in the poetry of Auden, Lewis, MacDiarmid, L.M., and Spender' [Dissertation, Pennsylvania University]

C127	April	Essays in criticism	pp227–236 M. A. M. Roberts 'Snow: an answer to Mr. Cragg'
C128	May	Poetry (Chicago)	pp101–105 I. L. Salomon 'An Irish oracle at Delphi'
C129	May 18	The Times	p10 rev. 'Apollo Society Recital' (organised by L.M.)
C130	July	Essays in criticism	pp333–7 D. J. Enright; pp373–9 F. W. Bateson; pp339–40 S. W. Dawson *on* 'Snow'
C131	July 5	The Times	p11 rev. broadcast 'Autumn Sequel'
C132	September 24	The Times	p8 rev. broadcast 'Prisoner's journey'
C133	November 20	The Times	p8 rev. 'Autumn Sequel'
C134	November 26	T.L.S.	p754 rev. 'Autumn Sequel'
C135	December 10	T.L.S.	p801 leader 'Poems with pictures' [Ariel series]

1955

C136 'Feats on the fjord' *in* 'Selected criticism; prose and poetry' Pub. Noonday, pp48–51

1956

| C137 | March/April | Poetry London—New York | pp40–2 Louise Bogan rev. 'Autumn Sequel' |
| C138 | November 23 | T.L.S. | pxv rev. 'The sixpence that rolled away' |

1957

| C139 | March 26 | The Times | p3 rev. 'Traitors in our way' |
| C140 | June 7 | T.L.S. | p350 rev. 'Visitations' |

C141	June 14	The Spectator	pp786–7 R. Conquest rev. 'Visitations'
C142	August 16	T.L.S.	pxxxi 'Divided loyalties in Ireland'
C143	November	Explicator No. 2	Item 10 Sister M. M. Barry 'M's 'Snow''

1958

C144 'L.M.' *in* 'Reviewers A.B.C.' by Conrad Aiken. Pub. Meridien Books. pp285–8

C145	January 1	The Times	pp4 & 5 'C.B.E. award'
C146	January 2	T.L.S.	p4 rev. 'New Poems 1958'
C147	July 4	Commonweal	p357 J. Fiscalini 'Sympathetic poet'
C148	August	Poetry (Chicago)	pp318–29 Samuel French Morse 'Transatlantic view'
C149	September	Voices	pp57–8 John Fandel rev. 'Visitations'
C150	October	Essays in criticism	pp393–404 M. Borroff 'What a poem is: for instance "Snow"'

1959

C151 'Evasive honesty: the poetry of L.M.' *in* 'Vision and rhetoric' by G. S. Fraser. Pub. Faber pp. 193–201

C152 Anthony Thwaite 'Contemporary English poetry' Pub. Heinemann pp85–89

C153	February 8	New York Times Book Review	p10 'With a moralising public tone'
C154	February 27	T.L.S.	p114 rev. 'Eighty-Five Poems'
C155	March 8	The Observer	p23 A. Alvarez 'Eighty-Five Poems'

C156	April	Essays in criticism	pp209–11 P. A. W. Collins and R. Draper 'Miss Borroff on "Snow"'
C157	August 6	The Times	p11 rev. 'Eighty-Five Poems'
C158	October	London Magazine	p71 et seq Alan Ross rev. 'Eighty-Five Poems'
C159	December 9	The Times	p4 rev. production 'They met on Good Friday'

1960

C160 Ottlie S. Stafford 'A critical appraisal of the works of L.M.' (Dissertation Abstracts XXI pp904–5. Boston University)

C161	September 7	The Times	p16 rev. production 'Another part of the sea'
C162	September 9	The Spectator	p376 rev. production 'Another part of the sea'
C163	November 2	The Times	p5 (Notice of Guiness Poetry Award 1960, 3rd. prize for 'Reflections')

1961

C164	?	Vinduet No. 1	pp227–32 Ellinor Lervik 'Med mitt sinns seks sylindre. Lyriken Louis MacNeice'
C165	March 11	The Times	p3 rev. production 'The Administrator'
C166	March 31	T.L.S.	p199 rev. 'Solstices'
C167	Autumn	Minnesota Review	pp118–129 D. W. Baker rev. 'Eighty-Five Poems'
C168	September 28	The Times	p15 rev. 'Solstices'
C169	November 12	New York Times	p4 M. L. Rosenthal 'Everything is subject for good talk'

1963

C170 'L.M.: a memorial address delivered at All Souls, Langham Place on October 17' by W. H. Auden. Privately printed by Faber.

C171 'L.M.' *in* 'Previous convictions' by Cyril Connolly pp320–3 Pub. N.Y., Harper

C172 'Poets today: L.M.' *in* 'T.L.S. Volume 2' pp128–30

C173	March	Poetry (Chicago)	pp424–6 Haydon Carruth rev. 'Uses of typology' [Solstices]
C174	September 4	The Guardian	p2 Obituary.
C175	September 4	The Times	p14 Obituary
C176	September 5	The Times	p14 T. S. Eliot letter
C177	September 6	New Statesman	p294 Philip Larkin 'Memoranda to Horace'
C178	September 7	Saturday Review	p251 Stephen Spender 'Songs of an unsung classicist'
C179	September 9	The Times	p12 Funeral
C180	September 19	The Times	p16 rev. production 'Persons from Porlock'
C181	September 23	New York Times Book Review	p38 Walter Allen 'London literary letter'
C182	September 27	T.L.S.	p746 rev. 'The burning perch'
C183	October 24	The Listener	p646 [extract from Auden's memorial address]
C184	October 26	New Republic	pp19–21 R. E. Elman 'Legacy of L.M.'
C185	November	Encounter	pp48–9 W. H. Auden 'L.M.'
C186	November	London Magazine	pp62–6 Ian Hamilton 'L.M.'

C187	December 5	The Times	p17 rev. 'The burning perch'
C188	December 22	New York Times	pp4–5 M. Rosenthal 'Surrender to despair'
C189	Winter	Poetry Review	pp316–9 Robert Greacan 'L.M.: an appreciation'

1964

C190 Earl Forrest Hazard 'The Auden group and the Group Theatre: the dramatic theories and practices of Rupert Doone, Auden, Isherwood, L.M., Spender and Lewis' [Dissertation Abstracts XXV pp1913–4. University of Wisconsin]

C191 John Frederick Povey 'The Oxford group: a study of the poetry of Auden, Spender, Lewis and L.M.' [Dissertation Michigan State University]

C192	February	Poetry (Chicago)	pp330–3 X. J. Kennedy 'Underestimations'
C193	March	Landfall	pp58–62 L. Curnow 'L.M.'
C194	March	Yale Review	pp447–58 Thom Gunn 'Modes of control'
C195	April	Poetry (Chicago)	pp1–3 George Barker 'Memorial stanzas for L.M.'
C196	Spring	Dubliner	pp4–13 Douglas Sealey 'L.M.'
C197	Summer	Wisconsin Studies in Contemporary Literature	pp133–150 Justin M. Replogle 'The Auden group'
C198	June	Proc. and Trans. of Royal Society of Canada	pp147–63 Desmond Pacey 'The dance above the dazzling wave: the poetry of L.M.'
C199	[July]	Review 11–12	pp91–4 S. Wall 'L.M. and the least line of resistance'
C200	September	Poetry (Chicago)	pp375–8 William Dickey 'In the convention'

C201 October 2   N.S.N.   p500 Ted Hughes rev.
                                        'Superstitions' [Astrology]

C202 October 15   T.L.S.   p937 rev. 'Astrology'

C203 December 1   Library Journal   p4814 Irving Pearlman
                                        rev. 'Astrology'

1965

C204 Julien Gitzen 'The poet as "Educated ordinary man": the poetic theory and practice of L.M.' [Dissertation Abstracts XXVI p3337 Wisconsin University]

C205 'L.M. at Marlborough and Oxford' by John Hilton *in* 'The strings are false' pp239–284 [see A36]

C206 John Press 'L.M.' (Writers and their work 187) Longmans for the British Council

C207 February 20   The Times   p12 [L.M.'s will]

C208 March   Poetry (Chicago)   pp404–5 Samuel French
                                        Morse 'Ends and means'

C209 March 11   New York Times   pp10–12 Robert Mazzoco
                    Book Review   'White goddess and black
                                        sheep'

C210 November 14   Sunday Times   p49 Christopher Ricks
                                        'M. in 1940'

C211 November 25   The Listener   p865 Stephen Wall rev.
                                        'Strings are False and
                                        Varieties of Parable'

C212 November 26   The Spectator   pp714–5 John Davenport
                                        rev. 'Louis' (Strings are
                                        False; Varieties of Parable)

C213 December 3   N.S.N.   pp886 & 888 V. S.
                                        Pritchett rev. 'Bog
                                        asphodel' (Strings are
                                        False; Varieties of Parable)

1966

C214 February   Critique   pp131–49 Serge Fauchereau
                                        'L.M.: un poète pendant
                                        les annes 30; un poète de la
                                        radio'

Items about Louis MacNeice

C215	February 3	T.L.S.	p81 rev. 'Strings are False; Varieties of Parable'
C216	Spring	Poetry Review	p27 N. Dugdale 'L.M.' (poem)
C217	November	Encounter	pp49–55 John Wain 'M as critic'
C218	November	Review of English Studies	p.450 A. D. Nuttall rev. 'Varieties of Parable'
C219	November 21	National Observer	p23 rev. 'Strings are False'
C220	December 11	Books Today	p4 C. Cole rev. 'Strings are False'
C221	December 17	America	p810 F. Caliri rev. 'Strings are False'

1967

C222	January	London Magazine	pp57–65 Rayner Heppenstal 'A demise of poets'
C223	January 28	New Republic	pp32–4 Stephen Spender 'Brilliant Mr. MacNeice'
C224	March 11	New Yorker	p192 rev. 'Collected Poems'
C225	March 24	The Spectator	p342 C. B. Cox rev. 'Collected Poems'
C226	April	Hollins Critic	pp1–11 William J. Smith 'The black clock; the poetic achievement of L.M.'
C227	April 7	N.S.N.	p479 Julian Symons rev. 'Collected Poems'
C228	Spring	Critical Quarterly	pp9–17 G. Hough 'MacNeice and Auden'
C229	Spring	Dublin Magazine	pp68–74 M. Longley 'A misrepresented poet'
C230	May 12	Commonweal	p240 B. C. Bach rev. 'Collected Poems'

C231 May 18	New York Times Book Review	p31 M. Bewley rev. 'Good manners' [Collected Poems]
C232 Summer	Yale Review	pp274–84 Louis Martz 'Recent poetry'
C233 December 1	Commonweal	p314 Julian Symons rev. 'Strings are False'
C234 Winter	Eire—Ireland	pp126–39 Sean McMahon 'A heart that leaps to a fife band: the Irish poems of L.M.'

1968

C235 February	Explicator 26	Item 48 John I. Cope 'M's Perseus'
C236 Spring	Library Chronicle (University of Texas	pp50–55 F. G. Stoddard 'The L.M. collection'
C237 July	University of Toronto Quarterly	pp338–58 A. T. Tolley 'The thirties poets at Oxford'
C238 August	Dissertation Abstracts XXIX	p590 Christopher M. Armitage 'L.M.: a biographical account and a study of his prose works' [Duke University]
C239 October	Twentieth Century Literature	pp133–41 John Gitzen 'L.M.: the last decade'
C240 October	Dissertation Abstracts XXIX	p1232 Richard Warren Pearse 'A study of the works of L.M.' (Columbia University)

1969

C241 'L.M.' by Walter Allen *in* 'Essays by divers hands Volume 35' pp1–17

C242 'L.M. and Stephen Spender: sense and sensibility' by A. S. Maxwell *in* 'Poets of the thirties' Pub. Routledge, Kegan Paul. pp173–202

C243 ? Western Humanities Review Volume 23, No. 2 pp159–171 Moya Brennan 'A poet's revisions: a consideration of M's "Blind Fireworks"'

C244 January 25 The Times p22 rev. 'Modern Poetry'

C245 October 9 The Listener p488 George Barker 'A proud and Roman judgement'

C246 November Columbia Library Columns pp36 & 40 K. A. Lohf 'Recent notable purchases'

C247 November Encounter pp70–4 R. Pocock 'The burning perch'

1970

C248 'Louis MacNeice' by Edward Elton Smith. Pub. N.Y., Twayne Pub. Inc. pp232

C249 April/June Bulletin of Bibliography pp51–2 & 48 William McKinnon 'L.M.: a bibliography'

C250 September Explicator Vol. 29 No. 1 Item 7 J. Darrill 'The riddle'

C251 Autumn Studies 59 pp253–66 Terence Brown 'L.M. 1907–1963: his poetry'

C252 December Notes and Queries pp467–8 Terence Brown 'M's 'Round the corner'

C253 Winter Contemporary Literature pp58–79 J. T. Irwin 'M., Auden and the art ballad'

1971

C254 'Apollo's blended dream: a study of the poetry of L.M.' by William T. McKinnon. Pub. O.U.P. pp.i–xiv 1–218 Bibliography pp219–229.

D

MISCELLANEA

MANUSCRIPT COLLECTIONS

GRAMOPHONE RECORDINGS

THE MANUSCRIPT COLLECTIONS

Note
The following gives only a brief outline of the major public collections. Where possible attention is drawn to published descriptions of individual collections.

University of Texas at Austin. The Library.
see Library Chronicle (University of Texas) Spring 1968 pp50–55. F. G. Stoddard 'The Louis MacNeice Collection'

PUBLISHED WORKS:
The library contains mss. for the following published works: One for the grave; Springboard; Holes in the sky; Ten Burnt Offerings; Autumn Sequel; Visitations; Solstices; The Burning Perch; The Dark Tower; The Mad Islands; The Agamemnon; Faust; selection of poetry 1929–41; The sixpence that rolled away; Meet the U.S. Army; The Poetry of Yeats; Astrology.
Some of the above are incomplete.

UNPUBLISHED WORKS:
62 radio and television scripts; 29 lectures; 2 plays (Eureka—Station Bell); 44 letters.
Also: 41 reviews; 55 articles and essays.

JUVENILIA:
Sherbourne Preparatory School; Magazine (3 numbers) and pamphlets c. 1920–1; Sir Galahad; Oxford Review; 6 essays at Oxford.

NewYork Public Library. The Berg Collection.
1. 'Blacklegs' (play) [First draft, 1939, accepted by The Abbey Theatre, but never performed]
2. 'The Conquest of Everest' [notes for the film]
3. 'Another part of the sea' [typescript of T.V. play]
4. Son et lumière at Cardiff Castle [outline of 1958 production *see* 'The Western Mail' 18th July 1958; 'South Wales Echo' 11th July 1958]
5. Mimeographed radio scripts.
6. Drafts of poems and lectures.
7. Books, various—in proof, draft, or signed copies.

Ohio State University. Columbus. Library.
[Columbia Library Columns November 1969 pp36 & 40 K. A. Lohf 'Recent notable purchases']
1. Essay on Sir Thomas Malory.
2. Correspondence with Mark Van Doreen.

Miscellanea

Lockwood Memorial Library. University of Buffalo. N.Y. State.
1. Notebook kept by L.M. while at B.B.C.
2. Poems in typescript.

BRITISH BROADCASTING CORPORATION. SCRIPT LIBRARY.

Date of first broadcast	Title	Length in minutes
1941		
15 February	Word from America	30
25 March	Cook's Tour of the London Subways	15
16 April	The March of the 10,000	15
5 May	The Stones Cry Out: No. 1—Dr. Johnson Takes It	20
27 May	The Stones Cry Out: No. 4—Westminster Abbey	15
2 June	The Stones Cry Out: No. 5—Madame Tussaud's	15
23 June	The Stones Cry Out: No. 8—St. Paul's	15
7 July	The Stones Cry Out: No. 10—The House of Commons	15
16 July	Freedom's Ferry: No. 10—Life on an ex-American Destroyer	15
1 September	The Stones Cry Out: No. 18—The Temple	15
6 September	Dr. Chekhov	35
29 September	The Stones Cry Out: No. 22—The Royal College of Surgeons	15
27 October	The Stones Cry Out: No. 26—Belfast	15
28 October	The Glory That is Greece	45
24 November	The Stones Cry Out: No. 30—The Barbican, Plymouth	15
30 December	Rogue's Gallery	30
31 December	Salute to the New Year	30
1942		
12 March	Vienna	60
22 March	Salutation to Greece	15

Date of first broadcast	Title	Length in minutes
1 April	Calling All Fools	15
12 April	Salute to the U.S.S.R.	15
26 April	Alexander Nevsky	60
10 May	The Debate Continues	40
14 May	Black Gallery: No. 1—Dr. Joseph Goebbels	15
30 June	The Undefeated (of Yugoslavia)	60
16 July	Black Gallery: No. 10—Adolf Hitler	15
26 July	Britain to America, No. 1	30
6 September	The United Nations: a Tribute	15
25 September	Halfway House	30
4 October	Salute to the U.S. Army	15
12 October	Christopher Columbus	?
25 October	Salute to Greece	15

1943

3 January	Salute to the United Nations	15
29 January	Two Men and America (script unlocatable)	
21 February	The Four Freedoms: No. 1—Pericles	15
28 February	The Four Freedoms: No. 2—The Early Christians	15
7 March	The Four Freedoms: No. 3—The Renaissance	15
14 March	The Four Freedoms: No. 4—John Milton	15
21 March	The Four Freedoms: No. 5—The French Revolution	15
25 March	Long Live Greece	30
28 March	The Four Freedoms: No. 6—What Now?	15
3 May	Zero Hour	30
10 May	The Death of Byron	15
18 June	Sicily and Freedom	15
21 June	The Death of Marlowe	45
4 July	Independence Day	45
3 September	Four Years At War	45
8 October	The Story of My Death (Lauro de Bosis)	45
8 November	The Spirit of Russia	55
17 November	The Fifth Freedom	30
31 December	Ring in the New (Year)	35

Miscellanea

Date of first broadcast	Title	Length in minutes
1944		
7 January	The Sacred Band	45
13 March	The Nosebag	55
23 April	This Breed of Men	60
30 May	D Day (no record of broadcast)	
28 June	He Had a Date	50
16 July	Sunbeams in his Hat	45
13 August	Why Be A Poet?	30
3 November	The Golden Ass	60
7 November	Cupid and Psyche	45
31 December	The Year in Review	30
1945		
10 January	A Roman Holiday	30
29 March	The March Hare Resigns	45
18 May	London Victorious	45
22 May	A Voice From Norway	20
1946		
21 January	The Dark Tower	75
1 April	Salute to All Fools	60
14 June	Poetry Promenade 14: Louis MacNeice	15
20 September	Enter Caesar	75
22 October	The Careerist	75
29 October	Agamemnon	105
2 November	Book of Verse 108: Louis MacNeice	20
16 November	Book of Verse 110: W. H. Auden	30
3 December	Enemy of Cant (Aristophanes)	90
13 December	The Heartless Giant	60
1947		
11 March	The Death of Gunnar (Icelandic Saga No. 1)	75
12 March	The Burning of Njal (Icelandic Saga No. 2)	75
22 June	Portrait of Rome	60
21 October	Autumn Journal: a selection	20
1948		
13 March	India at First Sight	60

Date of first broadcast	Title	Length in minutes
2 May	Portrait of Delhi: India and Pakistan No. 3	60
23 May	The Road to Independence: India and Pakistan No. 6	60
19 July	The Two Wicked Sisters	45
19 September	No Other Road	30
22 December	Trimalchio's Feast	?

1949

28 March	The Queen of Air and Darkness	100
26 August	Louis MacNeice reads a selection of his own poetry	30
30 October till 21 November	Goethe's Faust (in six parts)	8 hrs.

1951

15 September	Burnt Offerings (selections)	35
18 November	Portrait of Athens	60
11 December	In Search of Anoyia	45

1952

28 January	The Centre of the World (Delphi)	60
9 November	One Eye Wild	60

1953

6 January	Twelve Days of Christmas	60
31 May	Time Hath Brought Me Hither	60
5 July	Return to Atlantis	45

1954

31 January	Where No Wounds Were	60
27 April	Prisoner's Progress	90
28 June till 1 August	Autumn Sequel (in six parts)	30 each
15 October	Return to a School	30

1955

18 and 19 March	The Waves (in two parts)	60 each

Miscellanea

Date of first broadcast	Title	Length in minutes
3 July	The Fullness of the Nile	60
25 December	The Star We Follow (with Ritchie Calder)	60
1956		
5 February	Also Among the Prophets	90
17 June	Bow Bells	30
29 July	Spires and Gantries	30
8 October	Carpe Diem	45
30 December	From Bard to Busker	45
1957		
27 May	Nuts in May	75
22 September	An Oxford Anthology	20
24 September	The Stones of Oxford	30
1958		
9 January	Border Ballads	30
1 April	All Fools at Home	60
7 April	Health in their Hands	30
1959		
11 January	New Poetry	30
3 April	Scrums and Dreams	30
8 November	Poems by Tennyson	30
8 December	They Met on Good Friday	75
30 December	Mosaic of Youth	30
1960		
6 October till 22 December	The Odyssey (in twelve parts) MacNeice one of several translators	30 each
7 September	Another Part of the Sea (for B.B.C. Television)	
1961		
60 March	The Administrator	60
1 November	Poems of Salvatore Quasimodo	30
19 December	Let's Go Yellow	60

Date of first broadcast	Title	Length in minutes
1962		
4 April	The Mad Islands	75
1963		
24 March	Latin Poetry	30
9 June	New Poetry	30
11 August	Mediaeval Latin Poetry	30
30 August	Persons from Porlock	65
Posthumous		
10 June 1964	Eclogue from Iceland	20
27 January and 10 February 1966	Poems by Louis MacNeice (in two parts)	30 each

GRAMOPHONE RECORDINGS

1954 HOMAGE TO DYLAN THOMAS
Memorial performance recorded at the Globe Theatre, London, 24th January, 1954. L.M. Hugh Griffith, Richard Burton, Emlyn Williams.
Argo RG29
(*Requiem Canto* read by L.M.)
Also released U.S.A.

1958 JUPITER ANTHOLOGY OF TWENTIETH-CENTURY POETRY
Argo JUR OOA2
(*Conversation* read by C. D. Lewis)

1960 CAEDMON TREASURY OF MODERN POETS READING THEIR OWN WORK.
Record 2.
Caedmon TCO 995
(*Turfstacks, Refugees*)
Also released U.S.A.

1961 LOUIS MACNEICE READING HIS OWN POEMS
Argo RG196
(Conversation — Invocation — Carrickfergus — Dublin — The left-behind — The back-again — The gone-tomorrow — Apple

blossom—The cyclist—The nurse (i.e. The muse)—The truisms—Sunlight in the garden (sic)—The British Museum Reading Room—Bagpipe Music—Autumn Sequel (i.e. Autumn Journal IX)—Prognosis—Nuts in May—Brother fire—Rites of war—Death of an old lady—Christina—Meeting point—A toast—The Merman—Selva Oscure—Prayer before birth)
Also released U.S.A.
Sleeve note by L.M. ,who also prefaces some of the poems with information about time and mood of composition. The errors of the contents list on sleeve and record label are further confounded by the sleeve notes e.g. 'Sometimes recently I have tried to write very simply and starkly, as here in '*The wall*' . . .

1963 HERE TODAY
Jupiter JUR OOA6
(*The slow starter* read by Hugh Dickson)

1965 CONTEMPORARY BALLADS
Jupiter JUR OA10
(*The streets of Laredo* read by Patricia Kern)

1965 THE PATTERN OF POETRY. Part 9.
HMV CLP 1845
(*The sunlight on the garden* read by Redvers Kyle)

1966 POEMS OF LONDON
Argo eaf 109
(*Homage to Wren* read by Peter Orr)

1967 THE POET SPEAKS. Volume 9.
Argo RG519
(*Carrickfergus—Meeting point—Prayer before birth—Selva Oscure* read by L.M.)

U.S.A. recordings
L.M. READS FROM HIS OWN WORKS
Decca DL9141
(The muse—Conversation—Dublin—The left-behind—The back-again—The gone-tomorrow—Sunlight on the garden—Les sylphides—Christina—Bagpipe Music—Autumn Journal IX —The British Museum Reading Room—Meeting Point—Prognosis—The brandy glass—Apple blossom—Evening in Connecticut—Nuts in May—Brother fire—Death of a cat)
(Yale series of recorded poets)
Jacket notes by F. J. Warnke.

E

INDEX OF POEMS

A list of MacNeice's published poems, arranged alphabetically by title. In the case of variant titles the main entry will be found under the later title, with references from the variant titles.

In the case of composite poems e.g. The closing album, under the main title will be found a list of individual poems, and under these individual titles the publishing history of each poem will be found.

Abbreviations

a	anthology	
ACP	Poems 1925–1940	1940
AJ	Autumn Journal	1938
AS	Autumn Sequel	1954
BF	Blind Fireworks	1929
BP	Burning Perch	1963
CP	Collected Poems	1949
CP66	Collected Poems	1966
ded.	dedicatory poem	
EC	Earth compels	1938
EF	Eighty-five poems	1959
HS	Holes in the sky	1948
ICM	I crossed the Minch	1938
LD	Last ditch	1940
LI	Letters from Iceland	1937
OP	Out of the Picture	1937
OW	Other wing	1954
p	periodical	
P	Poems	1935
P37	Poems 1937	1937
PP	Plant and phantom	1941
S	Springboard	1944
So	Solstices	1961
SP	Selected Poems	1940
SP64	Selected Poems	1964
TBO	Ten burnt offerings	1952
V	Visitations	1957
*	recordings exist	

A cataract conceived as the march of corpses *see* River in Spate	
A classical education	ACP
A contact	p Spring 1935; P; P37; ACP; CP; CP66
Adam's legacy	BF
Address from my death-bed to Dr. Bruno, the concrete universal	a 1929
Adonis	BF
Aftermath	p June 1946; p Autumn 1946; HS; CP; CP66
After the crash	p Oct 1960; BP; SP64; CP66
A hand of snapshots (The left-behind; The back-again; The gone-tomorrow; The once-in-passing; The here-and-never)	p Dec 1954; V; EF (selection); SP64; CP66
A lame idyll	BF
Alcohol	S; CP; CP66
All over again	So; CP66
An April manifesto	p Oct 1934; P; P37; ACP 'April'; SP; CP; CP66
An eclogue for Christmas	p Apr 1934; p May 1934; P; P37; SP64; CP66
And love hung still	p Autumn 1938; LD 'Three poems apart, (for X); ACP 'Trilogy for X'; PP; p Jul 1941 'And love hung still'; EF 'First light'; CP; CP66
And the spirit returns	p Feb 1926
A night *see* Nocturne	
Another cold May	BP; SP64; CP66
Apollo on the Old Bath Road	p May–July 1926
*Apple blossom	p May 1960; So; CP66
April *see* An April manifesto	
April fool	V; CP66
Areopagus	TBO; CP66
A serene evening	BF
As in their time	BP; CP66
*A toast	p Christmas 1939; LD; ACP; PP; CP; EF; CP66

Index of Poems

Aubade	p Dec 1934 'Great expectations' P; P37; ACP; CP; CP66
Aubade for infants	HS; CP; SP64; CP66
Auctioneer's speech	p Xmas 1936; OP; ACP; CP; CP66
Auden and MacNeice: their last will and testament	LI
August	p Oct 1933 'August a la Poussin'; P; P37; ACP; CP; EF; CP66
August a la Poussin *see* August	
Autobiography	p Sep 1941; PP; ACP; CP; EF; SP64; CP66
Autolycus	p 1946; p 1948; HS; CP; SP64; CP66
Autumn journal	p Feb 1939 'Canto II'; AJ; p Spring 1939 'Canto II'; a 1939 Canto VI; SP (selection); ACP; CP; SP64 (selection); CP66; *Canto IX
Autumn sequel	p Feb 1954 'Canto in memoriam'; p Jul 1954 'Love of women'; AS; p May 1955 'Canto XVIII'; CP66
Babel	S; CP; CP66
Babylon	p Nov 1924
Bad dream	p Jun 1960; So; CP66
*Bagpipe music	P37; p Jan 1938; ICM; EC; SP; ACP; CP; EF; SP64; CP66
Ballade for King Canute	ACP
Ballade for Mr. MacLeish	ACP
Ballade in a bad temper	ACP
Ballade of dirty linen	ACP
Ballade of England	p Nov 1940
Ballade on an old theme	ACP
Barcelona in war-time	ACP; CP; EF; CP66
Bar room matins	ACP; p Jan 1941; PP; CP; EF; CP66
Beginnings of a comic-delirious drama *see* Mahavveray	
Belfast	p June 1932; P; P37; SP; ACP; CP; CP66

Beni Hasan	p April 1956; V; SP64; CP66
Birmingham	p Feb 1934; P; P37; SP; ACP; CP; SP64; CP66
Birthright	BP; CP66
Bluebells	p Autumn 1946; HS; CP; EF; CP66
Books do not look at me *see* Sand in the air	
Bottlemeck	p Jan 1943; S; CP; CP66
Bound in stupidity and unbound	BF
Breaking webs	a 1928 and BF and p May 1929 'Impermanent creativeness'; CP; CP66
Bring me out of the cave	a 1940
*Brother fire	p Mar 1943; S; CP; EF; CP66
Budgie	p Dec 1962; BP; CP66
Business men	PP; ACP; CP; EF; CP66
But genius finds the commonplace a silver rhyme	p July 1926
Candle poem *see* Candles	
Candles	p Oct 1927 and a 1928 'Reading by candle-light'; BF and P37 and ACP and CP 'Candle poem'; EF; CP66
Canto XVIII	p May 1955; AS; CP66
Canto in memoriam: Dylan Thomas	p Feb 1954; AS; CP66
Canzonetta	p May 1953
Carol	HS; CP; CP66
Carpe diem	p Feb 1964; CP66
*Carrickfergus	EC; SP; ACP; CP; EF; SP64; CP66
Carrick revisited	p April 1946; HS; CP; CP66
Casualty of war, New York	p Spring 1941
Cats	So; SP64; CP66
Charon	p Nov 1962; BP; CP66
Chateau Jackson	BP; CP66
Chess	EC; ACP; SP64; CP66
Children's games	BP; CP66
Child's terror	BF
Child's unhappiness	BF
*Christina	p April 1940; LD; PP; ACP; CP; EF; CP66

Index of Poems

Christmas shopping	EC; ACP; CP; SP64; CP66
Circe ('Circe leans athwart')	p June 1925
Circe	p June 1932 'Vitreamque Circen'; P; P37; ACP; CP; SP64; CP66
Circus	EC; ACP; CP; CP66
Clock	p Jan 1940; p June 1940
Clonmacnois	LD 'Eastward again'; ACP
Clowns	EC; ACP; CP; CP66
Coal and fire	BF
Cock o' the north	TBO; CP66
Coda	SP64; CP66
Coming from nowhere	ACP
Constant	p Feb 1962; BP; CP66
Conventional serenade	BF
*Conversation	p Spring 1940; p Jan 1941; ACP; PP; CP; EF; CP66
Convoy	p Jan 1943; S; CP; EF; CP66
Corncrakes	So; SP64; CP66
Corner seat	HS; CP; SP64; CP66
Corpse carousal	BF
Country weekend	p Nov 1959; So; CP66
County Sligo *see* Sligo and Mayo	
Court historian	BF; ACP
Cradle song	p Nov 1925
Cradle song *see* Cradle song for Eleanor	
Cradle song *see* Cradle song for Miriam	
Cradle song for Eleanor	PP and ACP 'Cradle song'; CP; CP66
Cradle song for Miriam	a 1929 'Cradle song'; ACP; CP; CP66
Crossword puzzles	So; CP66
Cuckoo	p June 1935; P; P37; ACP; CP; CP66
Cushendun	p Jan 1940; LD; ACP; CP; CP66
Cushendun again	LD 'The sky is a lather of stars'; ACP
Cynicism	BF

Index of Poems

Daemonium	P37 'For services rendered'; EC 'Thank you'; ACP
Dandelions	So; SP64; CP66
Dark age glosses (on the venerable Bede; on the Grettir Saga; on the Njal Saga; on the Four Masters)	V; SP64; CP66
Darts	So; CP66
Day of renewal	TBO; CP66
Day of returning	p June 1951; TBO; EF; CP66
Death of an actress	p Dec 1940; ACP; PP; CP; EF; CP66
*Death of an old lady	p Sep 1956; V; EF; CP66
Death of a prominent businessman	p Oct 1924
Débâcle	p May 1941; ACP; PP; CP; CP66
Déjà vu	p Jan 1963; BP; CP66
Departure platform	p Jul 1938; LD; ACP; PP
Dialogue in Stornoway	ICM
Didymus	ACP; PP; CP; CP66
Didymus	TBO; EF; CP66
Dissolution of Valhalla see Twilight of the gods	
Dogs in the park	So; SP64; CP66
Donegal tryptich	p Feb 1955; V; SP64 (selection); CP66
Dreams in middle age	V; CP66
*Dublin	p Feb 1940; LD; ACP; CP; CP66
Easter returns	p Sep 1956; V; EF; CP66
Eastward again see Clonmacnois	
Eclogue between the motherless	EC; ACP; CP; SP64; CP66
Eclogue by a five-barred gate	P; P37; SP; ACP; CP; SP64; CP66
Eclogue from Iceland	P37; LI; EC; SP; ACP; CP; SP64; CP66
Ego see The individualist speaks	
Elegy for minor poets	HS; CP; CP66
Elephants	EC; ACP; CP; SP64; CP66
Elephant trunk	ACP 'Peripeteia'; CP; SP64; CP66

Index of Poems

Empty shoes	p Xmas 1936; OP; ACP; CP; CP66
Enfant terrible	p 1946
Entered in the minutes (Interregnum; Barcelona in wartime; November afternoon; Radio; Shopping; Business men; Night club; The lecher; The prospect; Didymus)	PP and ACP 'Octets'; CP; EF; CP66
Entirely	p May 1940; ACP; PP; CP; SP64; CP66
Epilogue *see* Postscript to Iceland	
Epitaph for liberal poets	p Jan 1943; S; CP; CP66
Epitaph for Louis	p Feb 1929
*Evening in Connecticut	p Sep 1941; ACP; PP; CP; EF; SP64; CP66
Evening indoors	BF; P37; ACP; CP; CP66
Everyman his own Pygmalion	p Jan 1933
Explorations	S; CP; CP66
Falling asleep	BF
Figure of eight	V; EF; SP64; CP66
Finale	p Xmas 1936; p Dec 1936; OP; ACP; CP; CP66
First light *see* And love hung still	
Flight of the heart	p Nov 1940; ACP; PP; CP; SP64; CP66
Flower show	p Jun 1960; BP; SP64; CP66
Flowers in the interval	TBO; CP66
For services rendered *see* Daemonium	
From down here	p May 1929
Galway	p Oct 1934; LD; ACP; CP; CP66
Garner melancholy	p May 1926; BF
Genesis	BF 'The universe'; ACP 'Kosmos'; CP; CP66
Glass falling	a 1928; BF; P37; ACP; CP; CP66
Godfather	p 1946; HS; CP; CP66
Goodbye to London	p Aug 1963; BP; CP66

Good dream	So; CP66
Great expectations *see* Aubade	
Greyness is all	BP; CP66
Half-truth from Cape Town	p Dec 1959; So; CP66
Handful of snapshots *see* A hand of snapshots	
Hands and eyes	HS; CP; EF; SP64; CP66
Happy families	a 1928; BF; ACP; CP; SP64; CP66
Harvest thanksgiving	p Nov 1926; a 1927; BF
Here is this strange room	LD
Hiatus	HS; CP; CP66
Hidden ice	p Mar 1936; P37; EC; ACP; CP; CP66
Hinges kill themselves	a 1930
Hold-up	So; SP64; CP66
Homage to clichés	p Feb 1936; P37; EC; ACP; CP; EF; CP66
*Homage to Wren	So; CP66
Homo sum	BF
Horses	EC; ACP; CP; CP66
House on a cliff	V; EF; SP64; CP66
Hymn of the collectors	OP; ACP
Hyppolytus of Euripidies *see* Translations e	
I am that I am *see* Plain speaking	
Icebergs	So; CP66
Iceland	p Xmas 1936; P37; LI; EC; ACP; CP; EF; CP66
Idealist	p Dec 1939
Idle talk	So; CP66
Il piccolo rifiuto	So; CP66
Impermanent creativeness *see* Breaking webs	
Inaugural rant	BF
Indian village	p May 1958; So; CP66
Indoor sports (Darts; Shove halfpenny; Vingt-et-un; Crossword puzzles)	So; CP66
In lieu	p June 1961; BP; CP66
Insidiae	p June 1935; P; P37

Index of Poems

In Sligo the country was soft *see* Sligo and Mayo	
Interregnum	p Jan 1940; p Mar 1940; ACP
In the cathedral (The voluptuary; The church warden)	p Dec 1926
Intimations of mortality	P; P37; ACP; CP; CP66
*Invocation	So; SP64; CP66
Jack and the beanstalk	p Mar 1926
Jehu	ACP; PP; CP; CP66
Jericho	p Oct 1960; So; CP66
Jigsaws	V; SP64 (selection); CP66
June thunder	P37; p Autumn 1937; EC; SP; ACP; p Jan 1941; CP; EF; CP66
Jungle clearance Ceylon	So; SP64; CP66
Kosmos *see* Genesis	
Laburnum	a 1929
Last before America	p Nov 1945; HS; CP; EF; CP66
Leaves from a journal	p June 1940
Leaving Barra	P37; ICM; EC; SP; ACP; CP; EF; CP66
Les neiges d'antan	p Xmas 1936; OP; ACP; CP; CP66
*Les sylphides	p Aug 1939; LD; ACP; PP; CP; EF; CP66
Letter to Graham and Anna	LI 'Letter to Graham and Anne Shepard'; ACP; CP; CP66
Letter to Graham and Anne Shepard *see* Letter to Graham and Anna	
Life of Lord Leverhulme	ICM 'Lord Leverhulme was a grocer's son' ACP
Littoral	p Nov 1945; HS; CP; EF; SP64; CP66
London rain	p Spring 1940; LD; ACP; PP; CP; EF; SP64; CP66
Lord Leverhulme was a grocer's son *see* Life of Lord Leverhulme	
Love of women	p July 1945; AS; CP66
Mahabalipuram	p Dec 1948; CP; EF; SP64; CP66

Mahavveray	BF 'Beginning of a comic-delirious drama'; CP; CP66
March gave clear days	p Autumn 1938; LD 'Three poems apart (for X)'; ACP 'Trilogy for X'; p Mar 1941; PP; CP; CP66
Mayfly	P; P37; ACP; CP; CP66
*Meeting point	p Christmas 1939; LD; ACP; PP; p Nov 1941; CP; EF; CP66
Memoranda to Horace	p Sep 1963 (selection); SP64 (selection); CP66
Men of goodwill	ACP
Middle age	BF
Moon fishery: a dialogue	p May 1926
Morning sun	P; P37; ACP; CP; CP66
Museums	P; P37; SP; ACP; CP; EF; CP66
Mutations	p Mar 1943; S; CP; CP66
Nature morte	P; P37; ACP; CP; EF; CP66
Nature notes (Dandelions; Cats; Corncrakes; The sea)	So; SP64; CP66
Neurospastoumenos	p Feb 1930
Neurotics	BF
Neutrality	p Mar 1943; S; CP; SP64; CP66
New Jersualem	p Dec 1962; BP; CP66
Night club	p Oct; 1940 ACP; PP; CP; SP64; CP66
Nocturne	p Oct 1925
Nocturne	BF 'A night'; CP; CP66
No more sea	HS; CP; CP66
Nostalgia	p Mar 1943; S; CP; EF; SP64; CP66
Notes for a biography	p April 1959; So; CP66
Novelettes (The old story; Suicide; Les sylphides; The gardener; Christina; The expert; Provence; The preacher)	LD; ACP; PP; CP; EF; CP66
November afternoon	p June 1940; ACP
Now that the shapes of mist	p Dec 1936; 'Poem' a 1937; P37; EC; CP; CP66

Index of Poems

*Nuts in May	p July 1943; S; CP; EF; CP66
Obituary	p May 1940
O'Connell bridge	p May 1940; ACP; PP
Octets *see* Entered in the minutes	
October in Bloomsbury	p Dec 1962; BP; CP66
Ode	P; P37; SP; ACP; CP; CP66
Off the peg	BP; CP66
Old maid	BF
Old masters abroad	So; CP66
Only let it form *see* The brandy glass	
On the four masters	V; SP64; CP66
On the Grettir Saga	V; SP64; CP66
On the Njal Saga	V; SP64; CP66
On these islands *see* The Hebrides	
On the venerable Bede	V; SP64; CP66
Order to view	p May 1940; ACP; PP; CP; EF; SP64; CP66
Our sister water	TBO; CP66
Paradise lost	p Feb 1929
Passage steamer	p Mar 1937; P37; EC; ACP; CP; CP66
Perchists *see* Trapezists	
Perdita	p May 1940; ACP; PP; CP; CP66
Peripetia *see* Elephant trunk	
Perseus	p Oct 1934; p Spring 1935; P; P37; ACP; CP; EF; CP66
Perspectives	p July 1961; BP; CP66
Pet shop	BP; SP64; CP66
Picture galleries	ACP; PP; p Winter 1941
Pindar is dead	p Xmas 1936; OP; ACP; CP; CP66
Place of the skull	HS; CP; CP66
Plain speaking	p May 1940 'I am that I am'; ACP 'The undeniable fact'; PP; CP; CP66
Plant and phantom	ACP; PP; CP; CP66
Plurality	p Jan 1941; ACP; PP; CP; CP66
Poem (even so it is not easy to be dead) *see* Nature morte	

Poem ('Just as those who gaze')
see The glacier
Poem see Now that the shapes of mist
Poem see Turfstacks
Postscript see When we were children

Postscript to Iceland	a 1937 and p Mar 1937 and P37 and LI and EC 'Epilogue'; ACP 'Epilogue to Iceland'; CP; CP66
Poussin	BF; ACP; CP; CP66
*Prayer before birth	p Jan 1944; S; CP; EF; SP64; CP66
Prayer in mid-passage	S; CP; EF; CP66
Precursors	S; CP; EF; CP66
Primrose Hill	p Aug 1939; LD; ACP
*Prognosis	p Christmas 1939; p May 1940; ACP; PP; p May 1941; CP; EF; CP66
Prospect	ACP; p Jan 1941; PP; CP; CP66
Provence	ACP; p Jan 1941; PP; CP; CP66
Radio	p May 1940; ACP
Ravenna	BP; SP64; CP66

Reading by candle-light see Candles

Rechauffe	BP; CP66
Reflections	p May 1960; So; SP64; CP66
*Refugees	ACP; PP; CP; CP66
Relics	p Winter 1947; HS; CP; EF; CP66

Remembering Spain see Autumn Journal Canto VI
Reminiscences of infancy see Trains in the distance
Requiem Canto see Autumn Sequel

Restaurant car	p May 1960; So; CP66
Return to Lahore	p April 1956; V; CP66

Index of Poems

Riding in cars	p Xmas 1936; OP; ACP; CP; CP66
*Rites of war	EF; V; CP66
River in spate	BF 'A cataract conceived as the march of corpses'; ACP; CP; SP64; CP66
Round the corner	BP; CP66
Rugby football excursion	EC; ACP
Running away from the war	LD
Sailing orders	EF; V; CP66
Sailor's funeral	BF
Sand in the air	EC and SP 'Books, do not look at me'; ACP; CP; CP66
Saul	p May 1929
Schizophrene	p Jan 1944; S; CP; CP66
Scottish love song	ICM
Seaside see The lugubrious, salubrious seaside	
*Selva oscure	p Aug 1960; So; SP64; CP66
Senescence	BF
Sentries	S
September evening	p Nov 1939
Shopping	p Dec 1939; ACP
Shove halfpenny	So; CP66
Sleep	p June 1932
Sleeping winds	p Mar 1961; So; CP66
Sligo and Mayo	LD 'In Sligo the country was soft'; ACP 'County Sligo'; CP; CP66
Slow movement	p Sep 1946; p Autumn 1946; HS; CP; EF; SP64; CP66
Slum song	p April 1946; p Autumn 1946; HS; CP; EF; CP66
Snow	p Mar 1935; P; P37; ACP; CP; EF; CP66
Soap suds	p Oct 1961; BP; SP64; CP66
Solitary travel	p June 1960; So; CP66
Solstice	So; CP66
Solvitur acris hiems see Translations a i	
Song see Sunlight on the garden	

Song in the back of the mind	p June 1927; BF
Sonnet	p June 1937; P37
Sports page	p Dec 1962; BP; CP66
Spring	p Mar 1926; BF
Spring cleaning	p Aug 1963; BP; CP66
Springpiece *see* Spring voices	
Spring sunshine	a 1929; P; P37; ACP; CP; SP64; CP66
Spring voices	p May 1934 'Springpiece'; P; P37; ACP; CP; EF; SP64; CP66
Star gazer	p Aug 1963; BP; CP66
Straight words to a crooked poet	p Sep 1942
Street scene	p Winter 1947; HS; CP; EF; CP66
Stylite	p May 1940; p Spring 1941; ACP; PP; CP; SP64; CP66
Suicide	LD; ACP; PP
Suite for recorders	TBO; CP66
Sunday in the park	So; SP64; CP66
Sunday morning	P; P37; SP; ACP; CP; EF; SP64; CP66
Sunset	BF
Sunset conceived as a peal of bells	BF
Swing song	S; CP; CP66
Take me for your occasion and and mute machine	a 1940
Take away that bathos	p May 1929
Taken for granted	EC; ACP; CP; CP66
Tami cari capitis	HS; CP; CP66
Thalassa	p Feb 1964; CP66
Thank you *see* Daemonium	
The Atlantic tunnel	So; CP66
The back-again	p Dec; 1954; V; EF; CP66
The blasphemies	So; CP66
*The brandy glass	P37 and EC 'Only let it form'; ACP; CP; EF; CP66
*The British Museum Reading Room	p Jan 1940; p May 1940; LD; p Oct 1940; PP; ACP; CP; EF; CP66

Index of Poems

The bulletins	LD
The burnt bridge	V; SP64; CP66
The casualty	CP; EF; CP66
The church warden	p Dec 1926
The closing album (Dublin; Here in this strange room; Cushendun; The bulletins; Running away from the war; In Sligo the country was soft; Galway; Eastward again; The sky is a lather of stars; Why now it has happened)	LD and PP and ACP 'The coming of war'; CP; CP66
The coming of war *see* The closing album	
The conscript	S; CP; CP66
The creditor	p Spring 1935; P; P37; ACP; CP; EF; CP66
The cromlech	p Nov 1945; HS; CP; SP64; CP66
*The cyclist	HS; CP; EF; SP64; CP66
The daily news	OP; ACP
*The death of a cat	p Mar 1952; TBO; CP66
The death-wish	p Sep 1940; ACP, PP; CP; CP66
The dowser	ACP; PP; p Winter 1941; CP; EF; SP64; CP66
The drunkard	HS; CP; CP66
The ear	p Sep 1940; ACP; PP; CP; CP66
The exile	p May and ACP 'Three thousand miles'; PP
The expert	ACP; PP
The gardener	LD; ACP; PP; CP; EF; CP66
The gates of horn	ACP
The glacier	p Oct 1933 'Poem'; P; P37; ACP; CP; CP66
*The gone-tomorrow	p Dec 1954; V; EF; CP66
The grey ones	BP; CP66
The habits	p Dec 1962; BP; SP64; CP66
The heated minutes	P37; p Sep 1937; ICM; EC; ACP; CP; CP66
The Hebrides	ICM and EC 'On those islands'; P37; ACP; CP; SP64; CP66
The here-and-never	p Dec 1954; V; SP64; CP66

The humorous atheist addresses his humorous maker	BF
The individualist speaks	p Nov 1933; P; P37; ACP 'Ego'; CP; EF; CP66
The introduction	BP ;SP64; CP66
The island	TBO; CP66
The jingles of the morning	p Xmas 1936; OP; ACP; CP; CP66
The kingdom	CP; EF; CP66
The knowledge without process	a 1940
The lake in the park	So; SP64; CP66
The lecher	ACP
*The left-behind	p Dec 1954; V; EF; CP66
The libertine	p Jan 1944; S; CP; EF; CP66
The lilacs and the roses *see* Translations c i	
The lugubrious, salubrious seaside	p Oct 1926 'Seaside'; BF
*The merman *see* Visitations	
The messiah	So; CP66
The mixer	p June 1944; S; CP; SP64; CP66
The muse *see* Visitations	
The National Gallery	p June 1948; HS; CP; CP66
The news reel	S; CP; CP66
The North Sea	p Sep 1948; CP; CP66
The old story	LD 'The old story is true'; ACP; PP; CP; CP66
The once-in-passing	p Dec 1954; V; SP64; CP66
The oracle	OP; ACP; CP; CP66
The other wing	OW; EF; SP64; CP66
The pale panther	BP; CP66
The park	So; SP64; CP66
The preacher	p July 1940; ACP; PP; CP; CP66
The prodigal son	p May 1930
The rest house	p Apr 1956; V; CP66
The return	p May 1940; ACP; p Feb 1941; PP; CP; CP66
The revenant	S; CP; EF; CP66
The riddle	EF; V; CP66
The satirist	p June 1944; S; CP; CP66
The sea	BF
The sea	So; SP64; CP66
The sense of smell	ACP; p Jan 1941

Index of Poems   129

The sky is a lather of stars *see* Cushendun again	
*The slow starter	p Mar 1961; So; SP64; CP66
The snow man	V; CP66
The springboard	p Oct 1942; p Mar 1943; S; CP; EF; CP66
The Strand	HS; CP; EF; CP66
*The streets of Laredo	p Apr 1946; HS; CP; EF; CP66
The Stygian banks	HS; CP; CP66
The suicide	p Oct 1961; BP; SP64; CP66
*The sunlight on the garden	p Jan 1937 and P37 'Song'; EC; SP; ACP; CP; EF; SP64; CP66
The taxis	p Oct 1961; BP; SP64; CP66
The tree of guilt	V; CP66
The trolls	p July 1941; S; CP; CP66
*The truisms	p June 1960; So; CP66
The twins	p Mar 1943
The undeniable fact *see* Plain speaking	
The universe *see* Genesis	
The unoccupied zone *see* Translations c i i	
The voluptuary	p Dec 1926
The wall	So; CP66
The ways are green and and gorgons creep	p Nov 1924
The window	p Aug 1949; CP; EF; SP64; CP66
The wiper	p May 1960; So; SP64; CP66
The witch of Widdigofree	p Mar 1925
This is the life	BP; CP66
This tournament	a 1927; BF
This way out	S; CP; CP66
Three poems apart (for X) *see* Trilogy for X	
Three thousand miles *see* The exile	
Threnody	a 1930
Thyestes	p July 1943; S; CP; EF; CP66
Time for a smoke	V; CP66
To a communist	p Spring 1935; P; P37; ACP; CP; CP66
To Eleanor Clark (ded.)	LD

To Hedli (ded.)	S; CP66
To Hedli (ded.)	CP; EF; CP66
To Hedli (ded.)	V; CP66
To Mary (ded.)	BP; CP66
To posterity	V; CP66
To the public	V; CP66
Trains in the distance	BF 'Reminiscences of infancy'; P37; ACP; CP; CP66
Train to Dublin	p Feb 1935; P; P37; ACP; CP; EF; CP66
Translations:	
a. Three odes of Horace	CP66
i Solvitur acris hiems	p Nov 1937; EC; ACP; SP64; CP66
ii Aequam memento	CP66
iii Carpe diem	p Feb 1964; CP66
b. Four medieval Latin poems	CP66
i Jam lucis orto sidere (anon)	CP66
ii Corona virginium (Sigebert of Liege)	CP66
iii Ut quid iubes, pusiole (Godescale)	CP66
iv Meum est propisitum (Archipoeta)	CP66
c. Three poems in defeat, from the French of Louis Aragon	CP66
i The lilacs and the roses	p Summer 1943; p Oct 1945; CP66
ii The unoccupied zone	p Summer 1943; p Oct 1945; CP66
iii Richard Coeur-de-Lion	p Oct 1945; CP66
d. The legend of the dead soldier, from the German of Bertolt Brecht	CP66
e. Hippolytus of Euripidies	p April 1939
Trapeze	P; P37; ACP
Trapezists	p Jan 1938 'Perchists'; EC; ACP; CP; CP66
Tree party	BP; CP66
Trilogy for X	LD 'Three poems apart' (for X); p Mar 1941 'March gave clear days'; ACP; PP; p July 1941 'And love hung still'; CP; CP66

Index of Poems

Troll's courtship	p May 1946; S; CP; SP64; CP66
*Turfstacks	p Feb 1933; P; P37; ACP; CP; EF; CP66
Turn again Worthington *see* Upon this beach	
Τοωδ Εαυτον	a 1927; BF
Twelfth-night	HS; CP; CP66
Twilight of the gods	p Oct 1924 'Dissolution of Valhalla'; BF
Under the mountain	HS; CP; SP64; CP66
Upon this beach	p Jan 1933 'Turn again Worthington'; P; P37; ACP; CP; CP66
Utopia	a 1930
Valediction	p Apr 1934; P; P37; ACP; CP; CP66
Variation on Heraclitus	So; CP66
Venus's song	OP; ACP
Vingt-et-un	So; CP66
Visit to Rouen	V; CP66
Visitations	p Nov 1955; EF 'The muse' (vi) and 'The merman' (iii); V; SP64 (i, ii, iv, vi); CP66
Vistas	So; SP64; CP66
Vitreamque Circen *see* Circe	
War heroes	p Xmas 1936; OP; ACP; CP; CP66
Weekend	HS
Wessex guidebook	p Apr 1956; V; EF; SP64; CP66
Western Landscape	p Nov 1945; HS; CP; SP64; CP66
What is truth? says Pilate (ded.)	HS; CP; CP66
When clerks and navvies fondle	p Autumn 1938; LD 'Three poems apart' (for X); ACP 'Trilogy for X'; p Mar 1941; PP; CP; CP66
When we were children	S 'Postscript'; CP; SP64; CP66

Whit Monday	p Mar 1943; p June 1943; S; CP; CP66
Why now it has happened	LD; ACP; CP66
Windowscape	So; CP66
Wolves	p Dec 1943; P; P37; ACP; CP; EF; CP66
Woods	HS; CP; EF; SP64; CP66
You who will soon be un-recapturable *see* Sonnet	
Yours next	So; CP66
Γνωῦι σέανῖον	a 1927

GENERAL INDEX

Volume titles are in upper-case, other titles in italics. Only the authors have been indexed in Section C. Items in Sections A–C have been indexed to running numbers, those in Section D to page numbers. See Section E for an Index of Poems.

Abbey Theatre, The, A39a n., *104*
Administrator, The, A33, *109*
AGAMEMNON OF AESCHYLUS, THE, A4, *104, 107*
AIKEN, Conrad, C89, C144
Alexander Nevsky, 106
ALLEN, Walter, A10b, C181, C241
All fools at home, 109
ALLOTT, K. A., C24, C39
Alphabet of literary prejudices, An, B204
Also among the prophets, 109
ALVAREZ, A., C155
American letter, B128
ANDERSON, Wallace, C117
ANEY, Edith T., C126
Another part of the sea, C161, C162, *104, 109*
Answer to an enquiry, B52
Apollo Society, C129
ARMITAGE, Christopher M., C238
ASTROLOGY, A34, *104*
AUDEN, W. H., A6, A35, A40, C170, C183, C185
AUTUMN JOURNAL, A12, *107*
AUTUMN SEQUEL, A28, B246, *104, 108*
AYTRON, Michael, A27

BACH, B. C., C230
BAKER, D. W., C167
BARKER, Fairlie, C121
BARKER, George, C195, C245
BARRY, Sister M. M., C143
BATCHELOR, D., C1, C3
BATESON, F. W., C130
BAWDEN, Edward, A26b
Berg Collection. New York Public Library, *104*
BEWLEY, Marius, C231
BILEK, Marvin, A26a
BISHOP, John Peale, C68
Black gallery, 106
Blacklegs, 104
BLAKE, Lorraine, A26c n.
BLIND FIREWORKS, A1
Board of Education, A18
BOGAN, Louise, C63, C78, C137
Border ballads, 109
BORROFF, M., C150
BOTTERILL, D., C108
Bow bells, 109

BRADBROOK, H. L., C20
BRENNAN, Moya, C243
Britain to America, 106
British Broadcasting Corporation. Script Library., *105*
BRITTEN, Benjamin, A4a n., A5a n.
BROWN, Stuart G., C72, C92
BROWN, Terence, C251, C252
Buffalo University. Lockwood Memorial Library., *105*
BURHAM, D., C124
BURNHAM, James, C86
Burning of Njal, The, 107
BURNING PERCH, THE, A32, *104*
BURRA, P., C14

CALIRI, F., C221
Calling all fools, 106
Cardiff Castle, 104
Careerist, The, 107
Carpe diem, 109
CARRUTH, Haydon, C173
Centre of the world, The, 108
CHAPMAN, Frank, C8
Childhood memories, B318
CHRISTOPHER COLUMBUS, A19 *104, 106*
Cinema, The, B147, B150, B154
Clark Lectures, The, A37 n.
COLE, C., C220
COLLECTED POEMS 1925–1948, A23
COLLECTED POEMS OF LOUIS MACNEICE, A38,
COLLINS, P. A. W., C156
COLUM, Mary, C50
CONNOLLY, Cyril, C171
CONQUEST, Robert, C141
Conquest of Everest, 104
COOK, R. L., C104
Cook's tour of the London subways 105
COPE, John I., C235
Comment on the technique of G. M. Hopkins, B60
Countries in the air, A36 n.
COX, C. B., C225
CRAGG, R. C., C125
CRAIG, Maurice, C80
Crash landing, The, B212
CROWDER, R., C96
CUMMINS, P. D., C114

Cupid and Psyche, 107
CURNOW, L., C193

DAICHES, David, C73
DARK TOWER, The, A21, 104, 107
DARRILL, J., C250
DAVENPORT, John, C212
DAWSON, S. W., C130
D Day, 107
Death of Byron, The, 106
Death of Gunnar, The, 107
Death of Marlowe, The, 106
Debate continues, The, 106
DERMODY, Frank, A39a n.
DEUTSCH, Babette, C49, C81, C88, C115
Devil, The, B8
DICKEY, William, C200
Dr. Chekhov, 105
DODDS, E. R., A36 n., A38
DOONE, Rupert, A4a n., A5a n., B72, B76, C13
DRAPER, R., C156
DREW, Elizabeth, C61
DUGDALE, N., C216
DUPEE, F. W., C99
Dylan Thomas, B235, B265, B266, 110
Dylan Thomas: memoirs and appreciations, B234

EARTH COMPELS, THE, A8
East of the sun and west of the moon, A40
Ecrivain brittanique et la guerre, L', B185
EIGHTY-FIVE POEMS, A30
ELIOT, T. S., C176
Eliot and the adolescent, B201
ELLMAN, Richard, A16c, A16d
ELMAN, R. E., C184
Enemy of cant, 107
English literary scene today, The, B197
English poetry today, B208
ENRIGHT, D. J., C130
Enter Caesaer, A40, 107
Eureka, 104
EVANS, B. I., C40
Experiences with images, B211
Extracts from a dialogue on the necessity for an active tradition and experiment, B72 see also B76

FANDEL, John, C149
FAUCHEREAU, Serge, C214
Fifth freedom, The, 106
Fires of hell, B25
FISCALINI, J., C147
FITTS, Dudley, C43, C85
Four freedoms, The, 106
Four years at war, 106
FRASER, G. S., C151
Freedom's ferry, 105
From bard to busker, 109

Front doors of ivory, The, B29
Fullness of the Nile, The, 109

Gael force at Wembley, B311
Garlon and Galahad, B33
GITZEN, Julian, C204, C239
Glory that is Greece, The, 105
GOETHE'S FAUST, A24, 104, 108
Golden ass, The, 107
Golden Ass of Apuleius, B186
GREACAN, Robert, C189
Great summer sale, B313
GREGORY, Horace, C109
GRIGSON, Geoffrey, C34, C60
Group Theatre, The, A4a n., A5a n.
Guiness Poetry Award, C163
GUNN, Thom, C194

Halfway house, 106
HAMILTON, Ian, C186
HAWKINS, Desmond, C56
HAZARD, Forrest Earl, C190
Health in their hands, 109
Heartless giant, The, 107
Hebrides: a tripper's commentary, The, B86
He had a date, 107
HEPPENSTAL, Rayner, C222
Hetty to Nancy, A6
HIGGINS, Professor, B105
HILL, Douglas, A34
HILTON, John, A36, C205
HOLES IN THE SKY, A22, 104
Homage to Dylan Thomas, 111
HILTON, John, A36, C205
HOLES IN THE SKY, A22, 104
Homage to Dylan Thomas, 110
HOOD, Arthur, C10
HOUGH, Graham, C228
HUGHES, Ted, C201

I CROSSED THE MINCH, A9
In defence of vulgarity, B90
Independence day, 106
India at first sight, 107
In search of Anoyia, 108
IREMONGER, Valentine, C103
IRWIN, J. T., C253

JACK, Peter Monro, C47, C65
Jam of Aganippe, B13
JARRELL, Randell, C58
JEFFARES, Norman A., C100
John Keats, B140

KENNEDY, X. J., C192

Landscapes of childhood and youth, A36
LARKIN, Philip, C177
LAST DITCH, THE, A14

General Index

LEAVIS, Q. D., C52
LEHMANN, John, C48
LERVIK, Ellinor, C164
Let's go yellow, 109
LETTERS FROM ICELAND, A6
LIENHARDT, R. G., C87
Literature and the lively arts, B227, B228
Lockwood Memorial Library. Buffalo University., 105
LOHF, K. A., C246, *104*
London victorious, 107
Long live Greece, 106
LONGLEY, M., C229
Lost generations? B254
Louis MacNeice at Marlborough and Oxford, A36
Lyric Psalter, The, B113

MACAULAY, Rose, C36
McCORMICK, John, C122
MACK, Maynard, C59, C75
MacKINNON, William T., C249, C254
McMAHON, Sean, C234
MacNeice, Hedli, A39
MADELEVA, Sister M., C45
MAD ISLANDS, THE, and, THE ADMINISTRATOR, A33, *104*, *110*
MALONE, Louis, A2
March hare resigns, The, A21a, *107*
March of the 10,000, The, 105
MARTZ, Louis, C232
MASON, H. A., C16
MATTHIEWSON, F. O., C25, C116
MAXWELL, D. E. S., C242
MAZZOCO, Robert, C209
MEDLEY, Robert, A4a n., A5a n.
MEET THE U.S. ARMY, A18, *104*
MELLERS, W. H., C53, C77
MILLER, Liam, A39a n.
Ministry of Information, A18
Miss Ambergris and King Perhaps, B19
MODERN POETRY, A10
MOORE, D. B., 7
MORSE, Samuel French, C21, C41, C148, C208
Mosaic of youth, 109
MOSS, Don, A34b n.
MUIR, K., C83

New Poems 1958, B258
New Poetry, 109, 110
New York Public Library. Berg Collection., 104
Nine new caps, B299
No other road, 108
Nosebag, The, A21a, *107*
Nuts in May, 109
NUTTALL, A. D., C218

O'CONNOR, W. V. D., C107

Odyssey, The, 109
Ohio University. Columbus., *104*
One eye wild, 108
One for the dead, B320
ONE FOR THE GRAVE, A39, *104*
OTHER WING, THE, A27
Our god bogus, B34
OUT OF THE PICTURE, A5
Oxford Anthology, An, 109
Oxford Poetry 1929, B32
Oxford in the twenties, B137

PACEY, Desmond, C198
Parable, A, B76
PEARLMAN, Irving B., C203
PEARSE, Richard Warren, C240
PENNY THAT ROLLED AWAY, THE, A26a
PERSONS FROM PORLOCK, A40, *110*
PETTET, E. B., C123
PLANT AND PHANTOM, A17
Play and the audience, The, B91
POCOCK, R., C247
POEMS, A3
POEMS 1937, A7
POEMS 1925-1940, A15
Poet in England today, The, B118
Poetry Book Society, A29a n., A31a n., A32a n., B255, B280, B316
Poetry needs to be subtle and tough, B231
POETRY OF W. B. YEATS, THE, A16, *104*
Poetry, the public and the critic, B218
Poetry today, B57
PORTEOUS, H. D., C113
Portrait of Athens, 108
Portrait of Delhi, 108
Portrait of Rome, 107
POVEY, John Frederick, C191
POWELL, Charles, C54
Press, John, C206
Prisoner's progress, C132, *108*
PRITCHETT, V. S., C213

Queen of air and darkness, The, 108

RAINE, Kathleen J., C90
REED, Henry, C94
REPLOGLE, Justin M., C197
Return to a school, 108
Return to Atlantis, 108
RICKS, Christopher, C210
RIKI, A16d
Ring in the New (Year), 106
RITCHEY, J., C70
Road to Independence, The, 108
ROBERTS, Brian, C6
ROBERTS, M. A. M., C127
ROBERTS, Michael, C76

RODMAN, Seldon, C64
Rogue's gallery, 105
Roman holiday, A, 107
ROSENBERGER, Coleman, C101
ROSENTHAL, M. L., C169, C188
ROSS, Alan, C158
ROUNDABOUT WAY, A2

Sacred Band, The, 107
SALOMON, I. L., C128
Salutation to Greece, 105
Salute to all fools, A21a, 107
Salute to Greece, 106
Salute to the New Year, 105
Salute to the United Nations, 106
Salute to the U. S. Army, 106
Salute to the U.S.S.R., 105
SAVAGE, D. S., C98
SCARFE, Francis, C84, C91
SCHWARTZ, D., C11
Scrums and dreams, 109
SEALEY, Douglas, C196
SELECTED POEMS (1940), A13
SELECTED POEMS (1964), A35
SHARP, Nancy, A9, A11
SHAWE-TAYLOR, Desmond, C30
Sherbourne Preparatory School Magazine, 104
Sicily and freedom, 106
Sir Galahad, 104
Sir Thomas Malory, B66, 104
SITWELL, Edith, C9
SIXPENCE THAT ROLLED AWAY, THE, A26b, 104
SMITH, Edward Elton, C248
SMITH, Janet Adam, C31
SMITH, William J., C226
SOLSTICES, A31, 104
SOUTHWORTH, J. G., C62
SPENDER, Stephen, C7, C74, C178, C223
Spires and gantries, 109
Spirit of Russia, The, 106
SPRINGBOARD, A20, 104
STAFFORD, Ottlie, S., C160
STAGEBERG, N. C., C117
STAHL, E. L., A24d
Star we follow, The, 109
Statement, A., B94
Station Bell, 104
STAUFFER, Donald A., C105
STODDARD, F. G., C236, 104
Stones cry out, The, 105
Stones of Oxford, The, 109
STONIER, G. W., C37, C55
Story of my death, The, 106
Story of the 'Great Triobel' clan, B3
STRINGS ARE FALSE, THE, A36
Subject in modern poetry, B75
Sunbeams in his hat, A21a, 107
SWEENEY, John L., C61

SYMONS, Julian, C67, C227, C233

Talking about rugby, B261
TATE, Allen, C57
TEN BURNT OFFERINGS, A25, 104 108
Tendencies in modern poetry, B105
Texas University. Austin., 104
That chair of poetry, B281
They met on Good Friday, A40, C159, 109
This breed of man, 107
This is the life, B308
THWAITE, Anthony, C152
TILLER, Terence, C110
Time hath brought me hither, 108
Today in Barcelona, B98
TOLLEY, A. T., C237
Touching America, B152
Traditional aspect of modern poetry, The, B196
Traitor's in our way, C139
Traveller's return, B148
Trimalchio's feast, 108
Twelve days of Christmas, 108
Two men and America, 106
Two wicked sisters, The, 108

Undefeated, The, 106
Under the sugar loaf, B301
United Nations, The, 106

VAN DOOREN, Mark, 104
VARIETIES OF PARABLE, 104
Vienna, 105
VISITATIONS, A29, 104
VICTORY, Gerard, A39a n.
Voice from Norway, A, 107

WAIN, John, C217
WALL, Stephen, C199, C211
WALTON, Geoffrey, C33, C44
WANNING, A., C66
Waves, The, 108
Way we live now, The, B155
Westminster Theatre, A4a n.
When I was twenty-one, B279
Where no wounds were, 108
Why be a poet? 107
WILSON, Edmund, C17, C118
WILSON, T. C., C26, C27
Windows in the ink, B12
Woods to get lost in, B289
WOOLF, Virginia, C71
Word from America, 105
WORTHY, Angela, C12

Year in review, The, 107
YEOMAN, J., C112

Zero hour, 106
ZOO, A11